How to Be
SAVED
and How to Be
LOST

How to Be
SAVED
and How to Be
LOST

The Way of Salvation and the Way of
Condemnation Made As Plain As Day

Reuben A. Torrey

ANEKO
PRESS

We love hearing from our readers. Please contact us
at www.anekopress.com/questions-comments with
any questions, comments, or suggestions.

How to Be Saved and How to Be Lost
© 2022 by Aneko Press
All rights reserved. First edition 1923.
Revisions copyright 2022.

Cover Designer: J. Martin
Editors: Sheila Wilkinson and Ruth Clark

Aneko Press
www.anekopress.com
Aneko Press, Life Sentence Publishing, and our logos are trademarks of
Life Sentence Publishing, Inc.
203 E. Birch Street
P.O. Box 652
Abbotsford, WI 54405
RELIGION / Christian Theology / Soteriology
Paperback ISBN: 978-1-62245-763-2
Hardcover ISBN: 978-1-62245-806-6
eBook ISBN: 978-1-62245-764-9
10 9 8 7 6 5 4 3 2 1
Available where books are sold

Contents

Preface

The immediate purpose of this book is to make the way of salvation as plain as day to men, women, and children, with the expectation that many of those who read the book will see the way, will take it, will be saved at once, and will obtain eternal life immediately. The book goes out into the world for the same purpose that Jesus Christ came into it: *to seek and to save that which was lost* (Luke 19:10 AKJV). The average man or woman, even among well-educated people, does not know how to be saved.

When I was nineteen years old and a senior in Yale College, I was awakened to the fact that I needed salvation, but I was totally ignorant of how to get it. I groped in the deepest darkness. I had gone to perfectly orthodox churches every Sunday of my life ever since I was a very little boy; I had been years in the Sunday school and could quote whole chapters in the Bible. I had read the Bible every day of my life for six years and read it through at least once. I had taught a large Sunday school class, but I did not know what to do to be saved. I have reason to believe that what was true of me is equally true of the average man and woman and the average boy and girl today.

I have reason to think that these sermons, which are simply an exposition in language that any man, woman, or child can understand, can make the way to be saved so plain that anyone who wishes to know that way can easily find it. Anyone can understand what God has to say in His Word on this all-important subject. Many (especially men) saw the way of life and took it when these sermons were preached to my congregation. One man said to me one night a few weeks ago, "I am fifty-two years old, and I have been waiting to hear that sermon for thirty-four years." He took the Lord Jesus and publicly confessed Him; he was saved that night.

It is hoped that many who have unsaved friends will put this book in their hands, and that these unsaved friends will be saved at once. I hope also that some of my brethren in the ministry may be helped into a more effective ministry by reading the sermons compiled in this book. If any of them wish to borrow from these messages to enrich their own, they are heartily welcome to do so. The truth in these messages is not mine, it is God's, and His servants are welcome to it. Many preachers say to me, "I borrowed one of your sermons. I hope you are not angry." No, I am glad; that is why I publish my sermons. God grant that these messages may be even more abundantly blessed in this book than they were in the pulpit of the Church of the Open Door.

Reuben A. Torrey

Chapter 1

Why Jesus Christ Came into the World

This is a faithful saying, and worthy of all accepta-
tion, that Christ Jesus came into the world to save
sinners; of whom I am chief. (1 Timothy 1:15 AKJV)

Our first subject is one that has engaged the thoughtful
and earnest attention not only of theologians but also
of sociologists, historians, political philosophers, and reform-
ers for years. Some tell us, "Christ Jesus came into the world
to proclaim the great truths of the fatherhood of God and the
brotherhood of man." Others say, "Christ Jesus came into the
world to complete God's original thought in the creation of
man." Still others tell us, "He came into the world to reorganize
society on new lines, to establish a new form of human society,
the kingdom of God on earth." Not a few tell us, "Jesus Christ
came into the world simply to proclaim new ethical principles
by which men were to mold their lives."

But there is no need for us to speculate, guess, or argue as to
why Jesus Christ came into the world, for God Himself has seen
fit to tell us in the most plain and explicit words just why He did.
You will find God's own statement in 1 Timothy 1:15 (AKJV):

This is a faithful saying, and worthy of all acceptation, that Christ Jesus came into the world to save sinners. No one can mistake the meaning of those words. Listen again: when we stop to reflect upon the exact meaning and full force of this statement, it will seem incredible. These words unmistakably declare that it was an interest in sinners, in the vile outcasts, in rebels against God, in blasphemers, persecutors, perjurers, thieves, robbers, harlots, thugs, bandits, and murderers that induced the glorious Son of God to leave heaven's joys and glories and come down into this world. And these words furthermore tell us that Christ Jesus came into the world not to punish sinners as the holy executioner of God's wrath against sin, nor to study them as a great philosopher. No, He came to *save* them. Does it look credible that the Son of God should step down from the throne of His glory, lay that infinite glory aside, consent to enter this world through the lowly door of Bethlehem's manger, and leave it through the shameful and dreadful door of Calvary's cross to save sinners?

Christ Jesus came into the world to save sinners.

No wonder Paul felt it necessary to preface this astounding statement with these words: *This is a faithful saying, and worthy of all acceptation.* Paul knew that philosophers and thinking men generally would not be ready to accept this statement of the purpose of the coming of that infinitely glorious person, Jesus Christ, into this world. Therefore, he called their attention to the fact that as incredible as this statement appears to be, it was God's own word and therefore worthy of man's unquestioning, absolute confidence and all-acceptance. Yes, this is why Christ Jesus came into the world; this is the great central purpose of His coming – to save sinners. *Christ Jesus came into the world to save sinners.*

On Whose Behalf Was It That Christ Jesus Came into the World?

Notice on whose behalf it was that Christ Jesus came – on behalf of sinners. *Sinners* is not a nice word, and the reason for it is even worse than the word. Sin is the foulest, most hateful, most hideous, most loathsome thing in all the universe. Disease, leprosy, death, corruption, rottenness, filthiness, and all other repulsive and disgusting things are all merely inadequate types of sin and its hideousness and repulsiveness. The sinner is the personal embodiment of all this foulness, vileness, and repulsiveness, and yet Jesus Christ, the Holy Son of God, came into the world on behalf of sinners.

Men and women who were sinners and who were conscious of the fact seemed to be the only people in whom Christ Jesus took any interest when He was here on earth. He received sinners; He called sinners; He ate with publicans and sinners. He announced as His program, *I came not to call the righteous, but sinners* (Matthew 9:13 ASV), and again, *The Son of man is come to seek and to save that which was lost* (Luke 19:10 AKJV).

A very prominent, eminently respectable, and profoundly pious leader among the Jews came in a very deferential way to Christ Jesus one night to ask Him a few important questions, and Jesus practically slammed the door in his face by saying, *Ye must be born again* (John 3:7 AKJV). He would not even reason with him but kept saying, *Ye must be born again*. In the very next chapter, a loose, abandoned woman wandered His way, and He told her all about the water, which if a man drinks, he will *never thirst;* He told her about the true way to worship and about His own messianic office.

In Luke 18, a most attractive young man came to Jesus Christ. This young man had led an exemplary life, a life of morality and piety and generosity and culture. But Christ sent him away sorrowful with an uncompromising demand that he sell all his honestly gotten possessions and give the proceeds to the poor. And in the next chapter, Jesus told a notorious, money-grasping old sinner named Zacchaeus that He wanted to visit his house.

In the seventh chapter of Luke, Jesus Christ rebukes a very respectable, highly esteemed, and hospitable gentleman named Simon, and almost in the same breath tenderly says to a formerly disreputable woman of the town, *Thy sins are forgiven. . . . go in peace.*

His interest was with sinners; all His tenderness was for repentant sinners; His infinitely gracious invitations were for sinners. Oh, how wondrously kind and gentle He was to repentant sinners. But how merciless He was to moralists, to all who boasted of their own goodness, their religion, and their "righteousness." He stripped off the veneer of decency that covered the real rottenness within, and called them *whited sepulchres,* and *graves which appear not* – enclosures of rottenness, corruption, and dead men's bones, a *generation of vipers.*

> His interest was with sinners; all His tenderness was for repentant sinners.

Jesus Christ came to save sinners. Do you want Jesus to take an interest in you and save you? Then you must take your place before Him as a sinner – a commonplace, unadorned, unvarnished, inexcusable, self-confessed sinner. Not a respectable sinner; no, not a sophisticated sinner or a cultivated sinner; no, not an attractive sinner or an amiable sinner; no, just a plain, unadorned sinner – a poor, miserable, vile, guilty, worthless, hell-deserving sinner.

Did you know that more people are shut out of Jesus Christ's saving grace, pardon, heaven, and eternal life because they won't come to Jesus Christ as sinners – plain, ugly, wretched sinners? Far more people are shut out of heaven by the pride that keeps them from crying, *God be merciful to me a sinner,* than are shut out by the enormity of their sins or by the stubbornness of their infidelity. It is as true today as it was when Jesus Christ first said it to the moralists of His own day: *The publicans and the harlots go into the kingdom of God before you* (Matthew 21:31).

One night at a late meeting in Chicago, as I passed through the innermost inquiry room, a lady of substantial culture sat among the inquirers. This woman held two or three university degrees; she was a professional and one of the most highly cultured women who attended our church. As I passed by, she said, "Mr. Torrey, will you speak with me?"

I replied, "If you will wait a few moments until I speak to these poor creatures over yonder," as I looked toward some poor outcasts grouped together in a corner of the room. "I will come back and speak with you." These poor outcasts knew that they were sinners, and they accepted Jesus Christ. Then I came back to the lady, drew up a chair, sat down in front of her, and asked, "What can I do for you?"

She replied, "Mr. Torrey, I have not had a satisfactory Christian experience."

I replied, "I do not think you have had any Christian experience at all."

"Why," she replied, "I am a church member."

I answered, "Unfortunately, that does not prove anything. I am sorry to say that I have known many church members whom I could not believe were really saved."

"But," she said, "I am a Sunday school teacher."

I said, "Unfortunately, that does not prove anything. I am sorry to say I have known not a few Sunday school teachers of whose salvation I was not at all sure."

"But," she replied, "I am the widow of a minister."

"Well," I said, "unfortunately, even that fact does not prove anything. I do not read anywhere in the Bible that anyone is saved by marrying a pastor. Now, I do not believe that you ever in all your life came to God as a poor, vile, worthless, miserable, hell-deserving sinner – not essentially better than those poor creatures over in the corner."

She immediately straightened up, and her eyes flashed as she replied, "No, I never did, for I am not."

I looked at her and quietly said, "You are about as full of spiritual conceit as anyone I ever met."

She gasped out, "Mr. Torrey, you are cruel."

"No," I replied, "I am kind. It is not cruel, but it is kind to tell people the truth. Now, you are a physician, are you not?"

She said, "Yes, I am."

I said, "Suppose you had a patient who had a great big tumor, and you took a sharp knife and cut it out. Would that be cruel?"

"No," she answered, "that would be the kindest thing I could do."

"Well," I said, "you have a great big tumor of spiritual pride, and by the grace of God, I will cut it out tonight."

The woman had sense even if she was proud. She immediately dropped on her knees and came to God as a poor, vile, worthless, miserable, hell-deserving sinner, and she got a satisfactory Christian experience. But there are some of you who have never done it, and some of you who are determined that you never will do it. Well, you will, or you will spend eternity in hell.

Come, my good-natured, upright, polished, perfect gentleman; you must come and take your place as a sinner if Jesus Christ is to take any interest in you and save you. Come, my fine lady with your fair and attractive life, beautiful character, generous culture, winsome personality, and honored place in society; you too must come to your right place before God as a sinner if Jesus Christ is to save you. Yes, you must get down right alongside your sister from the slums, for *Christ Jesus came into the world to save sinners,* and He saves nobody else. Are you one? Are you a real, genuine sinner? If not, Christ did not come for you. We have thousands in our churches today who have never taken their places as lost sinners before Jesus Christ, and, of course, they have never been saved.

When I was pastor at Moody Church in Chicago, these words were engraved in the stone over the door: "Welcome to this house of God are strangers and the poor." I fear that motto kept a good many people away from that church. They preferred to go where the rich and cultured were especially welcome. But suppose that motto had read, "This church is for sinners." Would you like to have gone to that church? But if this church in which we meet tonight is to be a true church of Jesus Christ, it is for sinners: *Christ Jesus came into the world to save sinners.*

But while this great and wonderful text takes away all hope from the mere moralist, it says to every man and woman who is unwilling to come before Christ as a sinner, Christ Jesus is not for you; the gospel is not for you; the Bible is not for you; heaven is not for you. On the other hand, consider how wide this text throws open the door for all who are sinners and who know it. Yes, even for the vilest. Listen again: *This is a faithful saying, and worthy of all acceptation, that Christ Jesus came into the world to save sinners.* How many a man and woman there is today who says, "Christ Jesus is not for me; salvation is not for me; eternal life is not for me; the inheritance incorruptible, undefiled, and that fades not away is not for me." Why not? "Oh, I am so great a sinner," one might say.

Listen: *This is a faithful saying, and worthy of all acceptation, that Christ Jesus came into the world to save sinners.* Do you hear that? On behalf of sinners, Jesus Christ came into this world. Because you are just what you are, a sinner – a grievous, low-down, miserable, hopeless, helpless, hell-deserving sinner, Christ Jesus came for you. He makes heaven possible for you, salvation possible for you, and eternal life possible for you. *This is a faithful saying, and worthy of all acceptation, that Christ Jesus came into the world to save sinners.* As I speak, I think of a long, long line of men and women whom I have met in different parts of the world who seemed utterly beyond hope. They considered themselves beyond hope because they had gone so deep into sin and remained so long in sin, but they were led by the power of this text to put their trust in the Savior who came into the world to save sinners. Yes, *Christ Jesus came into the world to save sinners,* and He does it. And He can do it for anyone who comes as a lost sinner. But He cannot do it for anyone else.

What Was the Purpose of Christ Jesus Concerning Sinners?

We see, then, that it was on behalf of sinners that Jesus Christ came into the world, but what was His purpose concerning sinners? To save them. *Christ Jesus came into the world to save sinners.* As already suggested, He did not come into the world to punish sinners. Neither did He come to condemn sinners. He did not come to upbraid sinners. He did sometimes upbraid certain classes of sinners, but that was not what He came for; that was merely an incident. He did not come to reform sinners. That is a hopeless and worthless task; it is like painting the cheeks of a corpse; it will not keep the corpse from rotting. Jesus did not come to help sinners do better. Ah, friends, a sinner's case is so desperate that he needs something more than help; he needs something that goes far deeper than help. Jesus came to save sinners, to radically, thoroughly, and eternally save sinners. He came to save them freely, fully, and forever.

He came to save sinners from the guilt of their sins. There is a holy God, an infinitely holy God, and when a man sins once, he is a guilty sinner before that holy God. His sins avert the

> Jesus came to save sinners, to radically, thoroughly, and eternally save sinners.

8

face of that holy Being from him; his sin separates him from that holy God. The wrath of that holy God is kindled against him, even though that God loves him. Christ Jesus came into the world to save us from our guilt, to save us from the wrath of God, and to give our guilty consciences peace.

How did Jesus save sinners from their guilt? Listen to God's own answer to that question: *Christ redeemed us from the curse of the law, having become a curse for us; for it is written, Cursed is every one that hangeth on a tree* (Galatians 3:13 ASV). He saved us from the guilt of sin by taking our guilt upon Himself, by bearing our penalty in His own body on the cross of Calvary. The curse was your due and mine, but Jesus Christ, God manifested in the flesh, took that curse upon Himself. Listen again: All we, like sheep, have gone astray; we have turned everyone to his own way; and Jehovah hath made to strike on Him [that is, on Jesus Christ] the iniquity of us all (Isaiah 53:6, literally translated).

By His atoning death, Jesus Christ put away the sin that stood between you and God. By His atoning death, by the shedding of His blood, God's wrath at my sin and at your sin was settled, and settled forever. By His death, my guilty conscience finds peace. Let me say that this is not a mere matter of theological opinion with me, but a matter of glad and certain experiential knowledge. Christ Jesus saves from the guilt and penalty of sin; I know that. I do not merely think so or hope so; I know it. I know that Christ Jesus *hath power on earth to forgive sins* (Matthew 9:6 AKJV) because He has forgiven my sins, and they were very many; they were very great. And I know that through His atoning death, which I have accepted as the whole ground and the sole ground of my salvation, every sin of mine has been blotted out forever. I know that there is not a cloud between me and the infinitely holy God in whose presence the very seraphim veil their faces and their feet.

But Christ Jesus came not merely to save the sinner from the guilt of his sins and from the penalty of his sins, but *to save him also from the power of sin.* Jesus Christ does save from sin's guilt and from sin's punishment; He does save from a guilty conscience and from hell, but thank God, that is not all; *He saves from sin's power.* Our Lord's own words bring this out with great clearness and force. He says in John 8:34 (ASV), *Every one that committeth sin is the bondservant [slave] of sin.* We all know this is true. How many of us know from bitterest experience the slavery of sin, the slavery of drunkenness, the slavery of lust, the slavery of the greed for gold, the slavery of a bad temper, the slavery of an unruly tongue, the slavery of a mean disposition, or the slavery of unclean thoughts.

Yes, we have all known something about the bondage of sin, but listen to what Jesus Christ says two verses later: *If therefore the Son shall make you free, ye shall be free indeed* (John 8:36 ASV). Jesus Christ, the Son of God, the Savior who died on Calvary's cross to make pardon possible, rose from the dead and is a living Savior today. He has *all power . . . in heaven and in earth* (Matthew 28:18 AKJV), and is therefore able to save *to the uttermost,* not merely *from* the uttermost but also *to* the uttermost, all those who come to God through Him (Hebrews 7:25); He saves us from all the slavery of sin. He saves us from sin's power as well as from sin's guilt. That is what He came to do; that is what He does do.

Paul, who wrote the words of my text, knew from personal experience the power of Christ Jesus to save not merely from the guilt of sin, but to save from the power of sin as well. Paul had known the bondage of sin, the awful, grinding slavery of sin. He gives us a page from his autobiography in chapter 7 of Romans. He tells us of how he had found the law of God and how earnestly he had tried to keep it but how utterly he had failed. He had tried to break away from sin. The struggle as described in Romans 7 was a hard one, a determined one, but it resulted in utter failure. Paul tells us that the more he tried to break away from sin, the more helpless he found himself, until, at last in utter despair, he cried, *O wretched man that I am! who shall deliver me from the body of this death?* (Romans 7:24 AKJV). He felt like one chained forever to the dead, stinking body of sin, but when he cried, *Who shall deliver me from the body of this death?* he got his answer at once. You will find the answer in the next verse: *I thank God through Jesus Christ our Lord* (Romans 7:25).

Christ Jesus came into the world on behalf of sinners. He came to save sinners. He came to save them from the guilt, the penalty, and the power of sin. He does save whoever comes to Him and puts his trust in Him from the guilt, penalty, and power of sin. He will save any sinner who will believe on Him, who will just put their case in His hands. He will save them right now. He will not save anyone who will not come to Him as a sinner, but He will save at once, freely and fully and forever, every man, woman, and child who will come to Him and confess that they are sinners and put their trust in Him as their Savior from the guilt and power of sin. He will save them freely, fully, and forever.

Will you let Him save you? If any man, woman, or child goes out of here tonight unsaved, you will have no one to blame but yourself. *This is a faithful saying, and worthy of all acceptation, that Christ Jesus came into the world to save sinners.* Let Him save you right now.

Chapter 2

A Good Man Who Went to Hell and a Bad Man Who Went to Heaven

And he spake also this parable unto certain who trusted in themselves that they were righteous, and set all others at nought: Two men went up into the temple to pray; the one a Pharisee, and the other a publican. The Pharisee stood and prayed thus with himself, God, I thank thee, that I am not as the rest of men, extortioners, unjust, adulterers, or even as this publican. I fast twice in the week; I give tithes of all that I get. But the publican, standing afar off, would not lift up so much as his eyes unto heaven, but smote his breast, saying, God, be thou merciful to me a sinner. I say unto you, This man went down to his house justified rather than the other: for every one that exalteth himself shall be humbled; but he that humbleth himself shall be exalted. (Luke 18:9-14 ASV)

Some of you will think I have this subject twisted and that it ought to read, "A Good Man Who Went to Heaven and a Bad Man Who Went to Hell." But the subject, as I have given it, is exactly right. Jesus Christ Himself is my authority for saying that this "good" man went to hell and that this bad man went to heaven. He has given us the picture of this good man and of this bad man; Jesus Himself is responsible for the statement that the good man was lost and that the bad man was saved. Read our Lord's own words about it in Luke 18:9-14 (ASV):

And he spake also this parable unto certain who trusted in themselves that they were righteous, and set all others at nought: Two men went up into the temple to pray; the one a Pharisee, and the other a publican. The Pharisee stood and prayed thus with himself, God, I thank thee, that I am not as the rest of men, extortioners, unjust, adulterers, or even as this publican. I fast twice in the week; I give tithes of all that I get. But the publican, standing afar off, would not lift up so much as his eyes unto heaven, but smote his breast, saying, God, be thou merciful to me a sinner. I say unto you, This man went down to his house justified rather than the other: for every one that exalteth himself shall be humbled; but he that humbleth himself shall be exalted.

Jesus definitely declares here that *the publican . . . went down to his house justified,* and a man who is *justified* before God is saved; he is sure to go to heaven. On the other hand, Jesus Christ tells us with equal plainness that *the Pharisee* went down to his house unjustified, and a man who is unjustified before God is sure to go to hell. Now let us look at the two men of whom our Lord Jesus has drawn so graphic and so instructive a picture in a very few but very telling words.

The Good Man Who Went to Hell

Characteristics of the Good Man
We notice first that this man was a moral man, a clean man in his personal habits. He could look right up into the face of God who knows our every act, our secret acts, which are done under

cover of the night as well as our public acts which all see, and our secret thoughts, and he could say, "I am not an adulterer. I am a clean man morally." It is a good thing to be able to say that. Some of you men here could not say that. God pity you. You might say it to me, but you could not say it to God; you would not dare. But this man could say it and say it to God, and yet he was not saved.

A good many men in our day build their hopes for eternity on their outward goodness, on the fact that their actions have not been defiled by one of the most loathsome of all sins in any of its forms; their speech is clean; their conversation is generally pure, and they never read the vile literature so prevalent in our day. Well, outward righteousness is a good thing, but it won't save anyone, and if that is all you have to build your hope of heaven upon, you are lost and headed straight for hell.

We also notice that this man was honest in his business relations. He could look up into God's face and say, "I am not an extortioner," that is, a greedy, predatory money grabber. This man did not charge exorbitant rates of interest. He did not freeze other men out of business. He did not oppress his employees in their wages. He did not cheat his customers. It is a good thing to be able to say what this man said.

Many men here could not say what he said. Some of you found a man who was backed into a corner. You had a little money to loan, but oh, how you squeezed your poor brother. Some of you needed to have work done, and you found a poor, starving fellow. You hired him to do a dollar's worth of work for fifty cents, and even then, you called it charity. Some of you took advantage of a man's or woman's ignorance and charged them double for what you sold them and called it business enterprise, but God called it stealing.

Then, today many "eminently respectable citizens" build up great business enterprises by crowding someone else out. Their vast fortunes are built upon the ruined business enterprises of others, upon broken hearts and desolated homes, and God only knows what else. It is a great thing in days like these to be able to look up into God's face and say what this man said: "I am not greedy; I am not a money grabber; I am not an extortioner"; but it won't save you. This man could say it, but Jesus Christ says he was lost in spite of all that; he went down to his house unjustified – he went to hell after all.

A good many tonight have their hopes for eternity based on the fact that they are generally honest in business, that they believe in the "square deal" and practice the "square deal" themselves; but if you have no better foundation than that for your hope of heaven, you are a lost man.

Next, we notice that this man was a highly respected member of society. He was a Pharisee. The Pharisees were a highly respected class of society. They deserved to be. Everybody respected them. They were the one class of society that was held in highest esteem. They occupied a higher place in public esteem in Jerusalem than the members of any of our present civic organizations for moral and

Many men think God must think well of them because men do.

political betterment occupy today, and perhaps with better reason. When the ordinary citizen saw a Pharisee going down the street, he would say to his son, "There goes Mr. Simon Dikaios. He is a Pharisee, a very fine man, very upright, very pure, and always thrifty. I hope, my son, that when you grow up, you will be like him."

Now it is a fine thing to be highly respected. It is an exceedingly pleasant thing to be well thought of and to be well spoken of, but it won't save anybody. It won't keep anybody out of hell. It did not save this man. He is in hell now.

Many men think God must think well of them because men do. This is a great mistake, for Jesus Christ Himself tells us, *God knoweth your hearts: for that which is highly esteemed among men is abomination in the sight of God* (Luke 16:15 AKJV). God does not see as men see, for men look merely upon the outward appearance, but God looks on the heart.

I once heard a distinguished liberal preacher in Chicago speak when he was preaching a funeral sermon over a man who was an upright man but not a Christian. The brilliant liberal preacher wanted to make it clear that this man had gone to heaven. Under these circumstances, I heard him say, "Any world will welcome a good citizen," the intended implication being that heaven would welcome this man because he was a good citizen, even though he was not a Christian man. I am afraid this liberal preacher was not knowledgeable about the heavenly world and the conditions upon which one is welcomed there. Many citizens of Los Angeles, highly respected gentlemen like our friend the Pharisee of the text, do not stand the slightest chance of spending eternity in heaven unless they do something that they have never done yet.

Look at the Pharisee again. This man saw no flaws in himself but was the best man in the world in his own estimation. Speaking to God, he said, *I thank thee, that I am not as other men are* (Luke 18:11 AKJV). Literally translated, what he said was, "I thank thee that I am not as the rest of men." He divided society into two classes. He was in one class all alone, and all the rest of men were in the other class. He was good and all the rest of men were bad, and there he stands exclaiming, "I thank thee that I am not as the rest of men." He had a mighty high opinion of himself, but he went to hell just the same.

How many men there are who are building their hopes of heaven on their inability to discover any flaws in themselves. "I do not see what I need of Christ," many are saying. Or, "I see no great sins in myself. Jesus Christ may do for the drunkard, the harlot, the thief, and the murderer, but what do I need of Him?"

Well, let me tell you why you need Jesus Christ. You need Him to save you from being everlastingly damned. That is all, but that is enough, isn't it? You talk quite like this Pharisee who, our Lord Jesus tells us, went down to his house unjustified, was lost, and is now in hell.

Also, this Pharisee was a religious man. Every Pharisee was very religious, and this particular Pharisee was especially so. All Pharisees were often given to reading the Scriptures and other pious books. They were given to prayer and religious ceremonies. This particular Pharisee could tell the Lord how often he fasted every week; he fasted twice every week. He fasted far more frequently than the law required of him. He was also perfectly orthodox. The pharisaical party was the orthodox party. The Sadducees were the heretics. Now, religious ceremonies are good. Praying is good. Fasting is good. Orthodoxy is very good. But all of these put together won't save anyone; they won't keep anyone out of hell. No, in all this world's history, they have never saved one single soul.

Many depend upon these things as the foundation of their hope of heaven. "Oh, I am quite sure I will go to heaven," many are saying, "for I pray every morning and every night; I read the Bible every day; I go to church every Sunday; I fast on Fridays and through Lent. I partake of Communion very often, and I am orthodox in my creed, very orthodox. I believe in the verbal inspiration of the Bible, in the virgin birth of our Lord, and in the deity of the Lord Jesus. I believe in the literal bodily resurrection, in the atonement by the shed blood of Jesus Christ, and in the premillennial coming of Christ. I also believe in endless punishment. Oh, I am safe." Fine, very fine;

> Religion is a good thing, a very good thing, but many men and women will be in hell who were very religious on earth and very orthodox too.

but listen: All you have mentioned does not prove you are saved and headed for heaven. Religion is a good thing, a very good thing, but many men and women will be in hell who were very religious on earth and very orthodox too.

But we have not yet reached the end of the excellencies of this Pharisee. This Pharisee was a generous man. He could tell God he gave a tenth of all he made. It is a good thing to be able to say that. I wonder how many in this audience could say, "I give a tenth of all I get." I wish more of you could. I wish it for your own sakes. I wish it for the sake of the poor. I wish it for Jesus Christ's sake. It is a good thing to be generous. It is a good thing to give away one dollar in every ten dollars you make, ten dollars in every hundred dollars, ten thousand dollars in every hundred thousand you make. Yes, it is a good thing, a mighty fine thing, but it won't save you. It won't take you to heaven. This Pharisee did it, and he was lost after all. He went as straight to hell as many who never gave a penny.

Don't you think that this Pharisee was a pretty good man, as men go? Wasn't he in many important respects a most exemplary man? But he was lost! Jesus Christ distinctly tells us he went down to his house unjustified, an unforgiven sinner, under the wrath of God. He went to hell! Why? For precisely the same reason that many of you tonight are lost and on the road to hell.

Why the Good Man Went to Hell

First, he went to hell because he trusted in himself. In verse 9 we read that Jesus spoke this parable *unto certain who trusted in themselves that they were righteous.* This man counted his virtues, his clean life, his honesty in business, the high esteem in which he was held in the community, his own high estimation of himself, his religiousness, and his generosity in giving, and he put his trust in these good qualities of his own. But any man who puts his trust in his own virtues and goodness, and many righteous acts, or in himself in any way will be lost; he will spend eternity in hell, no matter how good he is.

Secondly, this man went to hell because he despised others. We read in verse 9 that Jesus spoke *this parable unto certain which trusted in themselves that they were righteous, and despised others* (AKJV). He thanked God he was *not as the rest of men, . . . or even as this publican* (ASV), who stood near him praying. There are many like this man, many here tonight. You despise the drunkard; you despise the rum seller; you despise the bootlegger; you despise the harlot; you despise the criminal. You think that you are different from all these, but God has plainly said in His Word that *there is no difference: for all have sinned, and come short of the glory of God* (Romans 3:22-23 AKJV). And God also says, *If we say that we have no sin, we deceive ourselves, and the truth is not in us. If we say that we have not sinned, we make him a liar, and his word is not in us* (1 John 1:8, 10). You will be lost unless you refrain from trusting in yourselves and despising others.

There is no pardon of sin possible without confession that we are sinners.

In the third place, and principally, this man went to hell because he did not acknowledge himself to be a sinner. There is not one word or hint of *confession of sin* in all his prayer. There is no pardon of sin possible without confession that we are sinners. No man who will not definitely confess himself to be a sinner will ever enter heaven. God tells us this over and over again in both the Old Testament and the New Testament. For example, He says in Proverbs 28:13 (AKJV), *He that covereth his sins shall not prosper; but whoso confesseth and forsaketh them shall have mercy.* If you will not take the sinner's place before God and confess yourself a sinner, there is no possibility of your escaping hell.

In the fourth place, this man went to hell because he did

not cry to God for mercy. He told God how good he was. He considered himself as a saint richly deserving God's admiration, not as a sinner sorely needing God's mercy and pardon. There are a good many like him. There are a good many men in Los Angeles who might have sat for this picture of "The Man Who Went to Hell," which our Lord Jesus has drawn in our text, and all such persons are lost. Every man is a sinner needing pardon, and no matter how good a man may be, or may think he is, he will never be saved; he will never get God's favor; he will never be pardoned; he will not escape an everlasting hell until he gets down before God and honestly cries to God for mercy.

It was a very simple way in which this good man was lost, just by not taking his right place before God as a sinner and crying to God for mercy; that is the way many of the best men and women in this house are being lost tonight. Wake up! Wake up, before it is too late! Wake up now, to the fact that you are a sinner, or you will wake up someday in hell! Cry to God tonight for mercy and for forgiveness of your many sins, or you will cry someday for a drop of water to cool your swollen tongue when you are in anguish in the flames of hell.

The Bad Man Who Went to Heaven

Characteristics of the Bad Man
In the first place, he was an immoral man. Without a doubt he was an immoral man, for the business he was in necessitated his being immoral. A man could hardly be honest in the business in which this man was engaged. He was a petty tax gatherer. The Roman government farmed out the taxes of a province as a whole, and the collector for the province had to get his money back as best he could by whatever means he could. In addition, he had to make a profit for himself. He farmed out his province in sections, and the collector of taxes of each section had to get

his share. This man in turn farmed out his section to the petty tax gatherers, the publicans, and they had to get their share. Extortion and crookedness of all kinds were employed to make the business of a publican pay. A man could hardly be honest in that business, and he was therefore an outcast from good society and classed with sinners. *Publicans and sinners* was the phrase constantly used concerning publicans.

Secondly, this man was looked down upon by his fellow men. While the Pharisee was the man who was universally held in highest esteem, the publican was the man who was universally held in utter contempt. Remember, though, that the fact that you belong to a class everyone despises is no proof whatever that you can never enter heaven.

And third, this man saw many faults in himself. In his own eyes, he was the *chief of sinners.* While the Pharisee thought of himself as the best man in the world, the publican thought of himself as the worst. While the Pharisee thanked God he was *not as the rest of men,* the publican regarded himself as *a sinner* (Luke 18:13), the one preeminent sinner.

The fact that a man sees himself as a great sinner, even the greatest of sinners, is no reason for his thinking he cannot get to heaven. Paul said, *This is a faithful saying, and worthy of all acceptation, that Christ Jesus came into the world to save sinners; of whom I am chief.* Yet Paul is in heaven today. When they cut off his head in Rome, his spirit departed to be with Christ in glory (Philippians 1:23). There will be a great company of men and women in heaven who saw themselves as the chief of sinners while here on earth.

In the fourth place, this publican who went to heaven had not been a religious man. The publicans were an irreligious, careless, godless lot. We see him in this picture becoming religious and going *up into the temple to pray,* but this was something new. He had been disdainful of the religion of his fathers, or he would never have been in the business of tax-collecting. Only the man who put making money before the religion of his fathers would consent to be a publican.

How often we look at the careless, irreligious crowd, the men and women who seldom or never go to church, who seldom or never pray, who never read the Bible, who have never been baptized or joined the church, and think there is no hope for that crowd. Oh yes, there is! This once utterly irreligious publican is now in heaven. There are hosts of men and women in Los Angeles tonight who never darken church doors, who will someday turn around and get to heaven if you and I do our duty.

I went to a lumber town in Wisconsin where there was not a single church, but where there were twenty-two saloons. I have spoken on the streets and in an old saloon and have seen a lot of these hard, old, irreligious tough guys saved, and the former keeper of that very saloon was saved. I have seen a tough, old sporting man, whose mother before him ran a sporting house in Omaha, and he had never been in a Protestant church before in his life. He started on that very day to spend the afternoon and night gambling, but he was brought into our church in Chicago and saved before he got out.

I have had a man call me out of this pulpit to speak to me under that gallery, a man who had been a gambler and a crook all his life, but he wanted to take Christ as his Savior and could not wait until I had preached my sermon. The irreligious gang is often more hopeful material to witness to than the self-righteous gang. A man may be as bad a heretic as this publican probably was; he may have been a foul, rampant, raging infidel or agnostic up to the present moment, and then get saved and start for heaven and eternal glory before this meeting is over.

I have seen a man who was an indecent and bitter infidel who had not been inside a church for twelve years. He had come into our building where he was saved before he got out. That man was preaching the gospel within a year.

One of the brightest converts we had in Kansas City while I preached there a short time ago was an intelligent university man. The first time he came to hear me he was an utter agnostic.

I once saw a man who was ninety-two years old and had not been inside a church for eighty years. He had come into a meeting like this, where I was preaching, and went out a saved man.

In the fifth place, this man who is now in heaven was a miserable old skinflint. Money was his god. He got all he could by hook or by crook and kept all he got. I admit that a man held in the power of the love of gold is almost the hardest man there is to save, far harder than a drunkard, a gambler, or a harlot; but it can be done.

Jesus Christ tells us this bad man went to his house justified, so beyond a doubt he went to heaven and is there now; he was certainly a tough customer, but he was saved. What did he do that brought him salvation in spite of all that was against him?

How the Bad Man Went to Heaven

First, he took his right place before God; he took his place as a sinner. That is what anyone must do and everyone must do in order to be saved. God's Word is as plain as day about that. God says in a passage already quoted, 1 John 1:8-9, *If we say that we have no sin, we deceive ourselves, and the truth is not in us. If we confess our sins, he is faithful and just to forgive us our sins, and to cleanse us from all unrighteousness.*

There is not a man or woman on earth who will ever get to heaven unless they own up to what God says in this Book, namely, that we *all have sinned, and come short of the glory of God* (Romans 3:23 AKJV), and get right down before God and confess that they are poor, miserable, vile, worthless, hell-deserving sinners. Jesus Christ can save sinners, even the worst, but He cannot save anyone but sinners – sinners who confess fully and frankly that they are sinners. Some of you here tonight will spend eternity in hell for that very reason – you won't own up that you are sinners. You know you are, but you won't admit it; you seek to conceal it or excuse it or gloss over it, and before you get through, you have tried to make out that you are a pretty good sort after all. Listen! You are bound straight for hell. You are taking the shortest and swiftest way to that awful place.

Secondly, this man asked for mercy. He saw there was only one hope for him and that was in the unmerited favor of God. Any man can be saved by grace. No one can be saved in any other way.

In the third place, this man recognized that there was no mercy to be had except on the ground of shed blood. That comes out in the literal translation of the words *be merciful*. Literally translated, it means "be propitiated." Listen, friends, there is no salvation or pardon except on the ground of the shed blood, the atoning blood, of Jesus Christ. God says,

> *Without shedding of blood is no remission.*
> (Hebrews 9:22 AKJV)

> *All have sinned, and fall short of the glory of God; being justified freely by his grace through the redemption that is in Christ Jesus: whom God set forth to be a propitiation, through faith, in his blood, to show his righteousness because of the*

passing over of the sins done aforetime, in the forbearance of God. (Romans 3:23-25 ASV)

Christ redeemed us from the curse of the law, having become a curse for us; for it is written, Cursed is every one that hangeth on a tree. (Galatians 3:13 ASV)

There is pardon, complete pardon, for the vilest sinner that ever walked this earth as a result of the shed blood of Jesus Christ; there is no pardon for anyone on earth in any other way. God knows I was vile – only as God and I know – but my sins are all forgiven. They are all blotted out. Thank God, I know that. If I should die tonight, I know my soul would be secure with the Lord, but it is only because of the shed blood of Jesus Christ. Nobody will ever get to heaven on any other ground. Our Lord Jesus Himself says, *I am the way, and the truth, and the life: no one cometh unto the Father, but by me* (John 14:6 ASV).

> There is pardon, complete pardon, for the vilest sinner that ever walked this earth as a result of the shed blood of Jesus Christ.

The Unitarian denies the atoning blood, and he will not and cannot get to heaven until he changes his position on that matter. The Christian Scientist denies the atoning blood, and not a Christian Scientist can get to heaven until he gives up that damning error. It is true, many call themselves Christian Scientists who are not really so; they do not realize that Mrs. Eddy denied and sneered at the atoning blood, but she did, so a real Christian Scientist cannot get to heaven until he recognizes his error on that point. Many of our professedly orthodox people today deny the atoning blood, so not one of them will get to heaven until they give up that damning error.

There is a way to heaven that is open to the vilest sinner that ever walked this earth, if he will simply recognize the fact that he is a sinner and accept God's testimony about Jesus Christ and His atoning blood; he needs to trust God to forgive him on the basis of the shed blood of Jesus Christ. Not one man or woman on earth can be saved in any other way.

A great number of you tonight are trusting in the very same things that landed the Pharisee of our text in hell, and unless you stop trusting in these things, you will soon land there too. You are neglecting to do what the Pharisee neglected to do, and you will wind up where he has already wound up, unless you change your course soon. But listen! The door of heaven stands open to anyone who will do what the publican did:

1. Take your place as a sinner before God.

2. Cry to God for mercy.

3. Recognize that there is no mercy except that based on the shed blood of Jesus Christ.

4. Believe God's testimony about that blood – that by the shedding of Christ's blood, your sins were all atoned for.

5. Trust God to forgive you and save you tonight, because Jesus Christ died in your place. Do that, and you are sure to get to heaven. Who will do it right now?

Everyone in this audience will leave this building justified or unjustified on the direct road to heaven or on the direct road to hell. It depends entirely upon whether you do what the Pharisee, the good man who went to hell did, or what the publican, the bad man who went to heaven did. It is for each one to decide for yourself what you will do. How will you decide?

Chapter 3

A Wonderful Contrast: Under the Curse of God or a Child of God

Which Are You?

For as many as are of the works of the law are under a curse: for it is written, Cursed is every one who continueth not in all things that are written in the book of the law, to do them. (Galatians 3:10 ASV)

But as many as received him, to them gave he power to become the sons of God, even to them that believe on his name. (John 1:12 AKJV)

What a sermon these two passages preach when placed side by side! They need little comment. They tell their own story and ought to produce their own effect.

All Who Are of the Works of the Law; Under the Curse of God

Let us look first at the dark side of the contrast: *For as many as are of the works of the law are under a curse: for it is written, Cursed is every one who continueth not in all things that are written in the book of the law, to do them* (Galatians 3:10 ASV). Every man who is *of the works of the law* rests under a curse.

Here a question of vital importance arises. What is meant by being *of the works of the law*? The context in which the words are found answers the question clearly and definitely. To be *of the works of the law* is to be seeking the favor of God and consequent salvation, life, and blessing by keeping the law of God and by our own good deeds. It is to be seeking the favor of God by our own righteousness, to be seeking "salvation by character." It is to be seeking salvation as something due to us because of our own righteous works, instead of seeking it as a free gift of God by the grace of God, the unmerited favor of God. Those who are *of the works of the law* are all those who are seeking the favor of God and His blessing and His salvation by their own good deeds, by their own righteousness, and by their own character.

All who are doing this are *under a curse*. Everyone who is doing this, every man and woman who is seeking salvation by their character on the ground of anything that you are or do, is *under a curse*. So God Himself declares this, in spite of all the reasonings and philosophizings of men, even though those men are leaders of thought in this "wonderful twentieth century," wonderful in the self-satisfied conceit of its scientists, philosophers, essayists, and novelists, if in nothing else. Listen again to God's words: *For as many as are of the works of the law are under a curse: for it is written, Cursed is every one who continueth not in all things that are written in the book of the law, to do them* (Galatians 3:10 ASV).

Next, why are those who are of the works of the law under a curse? It is perfectly proper for us to ask that question, and God has been pleased to answer it even before we ask it. It is answered right here in our text: *For as many as are of the works of the law, are under a curse: for it is written, Cursed is every one who continueth not in all things that are written in the book of the law, to do them.* The reason why those who are *of the works of the law are under a curse* is because the law, in order to get its blessing and the blessing of the Author of the law, that is God, demands absolute, perfect obedience. The law says, "Keep me perfectly and you shall be blessed; keep me perfectly and you shall live; but break me at any point and you shall die. He that does these things shall live by them, but cursed is everyone who continues not *in all things* that are written in the book of the law to do them."

There is only one member of the human race who has ever perfectly kept the law of God, and that person is Jesus Christ. So no man but Jesus Christ can find life by his own doing; no man but Jesus Christ can be saved by character. To talk about anyone but Jesus Christ being saved by character is to talk the sheerest nonsense. If any of us should keep the law of God perfectly, absolutely perfectly, from the hour of our birth to the hour of our death, we would thereby obtain the favor of God and win eternal life by our own doing, by our own character. But not one of us has ever done it. No human being but Jesus Christ has ever done it.

> So no man but Jesus Christ can find life by his own doing

The moment any man, woman, or child breaks the law of God at any smallest point, that salvation by character, salvation by our own doing, becomes an absolute impossibility. And every man, woman, and child has already broken the law of God at some point, and therefore if we are seeking God's favor by our own good deeds, by our own righteousness, by our own character, we are *under a curse.*

No man here can stand up and say, "I have kept the law of God perfectly. I never broke God's law at any point." There is not a man or woman here who has not only broken God's law but has also broken the first and greatest commandment of God at some time. What is the first and greatest commandment of God's law? Listen to our Lord Jesus' own answer to that question: *And he [Jesus] said unto him, Thou shalt love the Lord thy God with all thy heart, and with all thy soul, and with all thy mind. This is the great and first commandment* (Matthew 22:37-38 ASV).

Who can say, "I have always kept that commandment; I have always put God first in everything; I have always put God first in business, politics, home life, social life, pleasure, and study; I have always put God first in everything"? Who can say it? Be honest now; be honest with yourself, and be honest with God. You know you cannot say it. Every one of us has broken this great and first commandment.

There is, then, no hope for any one of us on the ground of the law, our doing, our own character or morality or merit. *For as many as are of the works of the law are under a curse: for it is written, Cursed is every one who continueth not in all things that are written in the book of the law, to do them.* If we cannot get out of the sphere of the law into some other sphere, the sphere of grace, we are doomed and will ultimately be damned.

How utterly foolish, then, is the man who expects to be saved by the law, by his own good deeds, and win eternal life by his good character or by his good deeds. *For as many as are of the works of the law are under a curse: for it is written, Cursed is every one who continueth not in all things that are written in the book of the law, to do them.*

Every man here who is counting on his own good deeds, his own morality, or his own good character to find favor with God is *under a curse.*

All Who Receive Jesus Christ; Children of God

Now let's turn to the other side – the bright side of the contrast: *But as many as received him, to them gave he power to become the sons of God, even to them that believe on his name* (John 1:12 AKJV). The first side of the contrast is very dark, dark as midnight, pitch dark; but this other side of the contrast is very bright, bright as the full noon sunlight of the eternal day. But every man who is *of the works of the law,* depending on his own deeds and his own goodness for salvation, is outside of Christ *and under a curse.*

On the other hand, every man who has thrown away all confidence in himself, his own doing and character, and has accepted Jesus Christ, is given the *power to become [a child] of God.* The word translated *power* in the Authorized King James Version of this verse means more than what we usually attribute to the word. It means the "authority" or the "right." The one who receives Jesus Christ, the incarnate Word of God, has not merely the ability to become a child of God, but he also has the God-given authority to become a child of God. It is the divinely bestowed prerogative of everyone who receives Christ Jesus to call himself a *child of God.* As John puts it in his first epistle: *Behold what manner of love the Father hath bestowed upon us* [that is, upon believers in Jesus Christ, those who have received Jesus Christ], *that we should be called children of God; and such we are* (1 John 3:1 ASV).

Only one condition is required to attain this immeasurably exalted authority – the prerogative and honor of becoming a child of God – and that is receiving Jesus Christ. Whosoever, anybody and everybody, receives Jesus Christ, the Son of God, instantly becomes a child of God. It doesn't matter what his past may have been; he may have been a very bad man or a very good man. He may have been a very religious man or an utterly godless and profane man. He may have been a very orthodox, intelligent believer in all the great fundamental doctrines of our faith, or he may have been an utter heretic or foul infidel. But the moment he receives Jesus Christ, he instantly receives authority to become a child of God. *But as many as received him, to them gave he the right to become children of God, even to them that believe on his name* (John 1:12 ASV). Any man or woman tonight can get the God-given right to become a child of God in an instant. All you have to do is receive Jesus Christ.

What does it mean to receive Jesus Christ? We need to be very clear and very sure about this. The Greek word translated *receive* means simply "to take" or "to take to oneself," to receive (or accept) what is offered. So to receive Jesus Christ means to take Jesus Christ to ourselves, to take Him to be to ourselves all that He came into this world to be to us.

What did Jesus Christ come into this world to be to anyone who would take Him? The Bible answers that question with great plainness and great definiteness.

First, Jesus Christ came into this world to be our sin-bearer, the One who bore our sins in our place to *pay the penalty of our sins.* We read in verse 29 of this same chapter from which our text is taken: *Behold the Lamb of God, which taketh away the sin of the world.*

> To receive Jesus Christ means to take Jesus Christ to be our sin-bearer, the One who paid the penalty of our sins for us.

To receive Jesus Christ means to take Jesus Christ to be our sin-bearer, the One who paid the penalty of our sins for us. Or as Paul puts it in Galatians 3:13 (ASV), *Christ redeemed us from the curse of the law* [that we were under, because we had broken it], *having become a curse for us* [in our place]; *for it is written, Cursed is every one that hangeth on a tree.*

In the second place, Jesus Christ came to be our Deliverer, not merely from the guilt of sin but also from the power of sin. In John 8:34, 36 (AKJV) we read, *Jesus answered them, Verily, verily, I say unto you, Whosoever committeth sin is the servant of sin. If the Son therefore shall make you free, ye shall be free indeed.*

So to receive Jesus Christ means to take Him to ourselves to be our Deliverer from the power of sin, to give up all our self-efforts to deliver ourselves from the power of sin, and just look up to the risen Christ, who has all power in heaven and on earth to deliver us from the power of sin.

In the third place, He came to be our divine Teacher and absolute Lord, who has a right to the absolute control of all our thoughts and desires and purposes and actions. In John 13:13 (ASV), our Lord Jesus is recorded as saying, *Ye call me, Teacher, and, Lord: and ye say well; for so I am.* Even in the Revised Version we don't have an accurate translation of the Greek in this passage. What Jesus really said was, "Ye call me **the** Teacher, and **the** Lord; and ye say well; for so I am."

So *to receive* Him means to take Him to ourselves as *the Teacher,* the one and only absolutely authoritative Teacher. He is the One whom we shall believe rather than the whole world. If the world (every philosopher, scientist, university professor, sage, and poet) says one thing, and Jesus Christ says another, we shall believe Him instead of them. We shall believe *the Lord,* the One who is our divine and absolute Lord to whom we hand over unquestioningly and unhesitatingly the absolute control of all our conduct in every area of life. We will bow the knee and *confess that Jesus Christ is Lord, to the glory of God the Father* (Philippians 2:10-11 AKJV).

When anyone receives Jesus Christ, takes Him to be his sin-bearer, and trusts God to forgive him because Jesus Christ made a full atonement for his sin by dying in his place and becoming his Deliverer from the power of sin, he becomes a child of God. When a person gives up his self-efforts to overcome sin, and trusts the risen Christ Jesus alone to give him victory over sin, he can call himself a child of God. Jesus Christ becomes his inerrantly authoritative Teacher, whom he will believe instead of the world, and to whom he unquestioningly and unhesitatingly surrenders the absolute control of all his conduct in every area of life. He will bow his knee confessing that Jesus Christ is Lord (Romans 10:9-10). The moment that anyone does this, that person gets the right and the authority, which God Himself bestowed upon him, to call himself God's child. Anyone tonight who will do this, can become God's child and become so at once.

We do not become children of God by praying, by reading the Bible, by turning over a new leaf, by quitting our sins, by doing good deeds, or by leading holy lives. As good as all these things are, we become children of God by the one simple act of receiving Jesus Christ, taking Him to be what He came into the world to be. *As many as received him, to them gave he the right to become children of God, even to them that believe on his name.*

Even if we have never been to church before in our lives, never read a verse in the Bible, or never said a prayer, the moment we receive Jesus Christ, we have the right to be *children of God.* Even if we have never done one single good deed in all our lives, and our lives have been full of sin and vileness every day, the moment we receive Jesus Christ, we get the right, the authority given to us by God Himself, to become *children of God.*

If Jesus Christ is not our authoritative and final Teacher and our divine Lord, we are not and cannot become children of God.

If, on the other hand, we go to church several times a week, read the Bible every day, and pray every morning, noon, and night, we cannot be children of God without Jesus Christ. If we give up every bad habit, give much to the poor, do all sorts of good deeds, and avoid all sorts of sins, but do not receive Jesus Christ as our sin-bearer and Deliverer from the power of sin, we cannot claim to be children of God. If Jesus Christ is not our authoritative and final Teacher and our divine Lord, we are not and cannot become *children of God.*

The right to sonship is in Jesus Christ, and you only get the right by receiving Him. If I put a thousand dollars in a package and then say to you, "Here, if you take that package you can have what is in it," if you took the package, you would get that thousand dollars, but if you did not take the package, you would not get that thousand dollars, no matter how many other great and good things you might do. Now, God has put the right to sonship in a package, and that package is a person, Jesus Christ. If you take Him, you get it; if you refuse Him, you cannot get it, no matter how many other good things you may do.

God makes this very plain in another place where He says, *He that believeth on the Son of God hath the witness in him: he that believeth not God hath made him a liar; because he hath not believed in the witness that God hath borne concerning his Son. And the witness is this, that God gave unto us eternal life, and this life is in his Son. He that hath the Son hath the life; he that hath not the Son of God hath not the life* (1 John 5:10-12 ASV).

Look squarely, seriously, and intently at the contrast: *For as many as are of the works of the law,* trusting in their own works and not in Jesus Christ, are out of Christ and have not definitely received Jesus Christ. All, even the best of society, without Christ are *under a curse.* But on the other hand, as many as receive Christ, regardless of the past, the vilest as well as the best get the authority to become children of God.

To which class do you belong tonight? I do not ask you whether you have been good or bad, moral or immoral, religious or godless, orthodox or heretical, but are you trying to get to heaven by your own puny "goodness" or by trusting in what Jesus Christ has already done? Are you *of the works of the law,* or are you of those who have received Christ and put their full faith in Him and Him alone? If you are of the former, God's Word says you are *under a curse.* If you are of the latter,

God's Word says that no matter what the past has been, you are His child tonight.

Under a curse! What an appalling phrase! How those words make a thoughtful man shudder. *Under a curse!* What curse? Whose curse? It is the curse of the law of God which you have broken, and the curse of the God whose law you have broken. It is the curse of the law of the infinite, omnipotent, omniscient, omnipresent, eternal, infinitely holy God, who made all the great worlds that go to make up our universe. This God upholds and absolutely controls that universe and all things in it; He holds the destinies of all individual men and all nations, the destinies of time and the destinies of eternity in His hand under the curse of *the God in whose hand thy breath is, and whose are all thy ways* (Daniel 5:23 ASV). *Under the curse of God!* It is awful. It is appalling. It suggests that solemn and terrifying word spoken by Jesus Christ Himself in Matthew 25:41 (ASV): *Then shall he say also unto them on the left hand, Depart from me, ye cursed, into the eternal fire which is prepared for the devil and his angels.*

Now turn to the other side of the contrast: *The right* [the divinely given right] *to become children of God.* How those God-breathed words make the intelligent heart bound and throb: *The right to become children of God.* Whose children? *Children of God.* Ah! What would it be for a ragged, starving street urchin to become a child of a king? But that is nothing, nothing at all in comparison with this – for you and me, moral derelicts such as we have been, sinners, poor and needy, weak and wounded, sick and sore, to become *children of God.* Not slaves, mind you, not servants, not retainers, not representatives, but children, *children of God.*

I thought it quite fine once when Mrs. Torrey and I had the privilege of sitting at the table three times a day for a week or two, right beside the son of one of Europe's reigning monarchs, the prince and his wife, the princess. But to be a *child of God!* Think of it! We cannot take it in, but I know that I am a *child of God.* Do you know that you are a *child of God?* You may become one and you may know it within five minutes. Listen: *But as many as received him, to them gave he the right to become children of God, even to them that believe on his name* (John 1:12 ASV).

Can it be true? Yes, beyond any question, it is true; God Himself says it. And it is not only true, but it is also open to you, open to any one of you; no matter how poor, ignorant, and wicked you may be, it is open to you right now.

Oh, men and women, young men and maidens, step out right now from *under the curse* of God into the glory of becoming *children of God.* What must you do? Only this: Receive Jesus Christ; that is all. Take Him to be your sin-bearer, and trust God to forgive you because Jesus Christ died in your place. Take Him to be your Deliverer from the power of sin, and trust the risen Christ, who has all power in heaven and on

> What must you do? Only this: Receive Jesus Christ; that is all.

earth to keep you day by day from sin's power. Take Him to be your absolutely authoritative Teacher and your divine Lord to whom you surrender the entire control of your life in all areas, and to whom you bow the knee and confess that He is Lord to the glory of God the Father. That is all. Will you do it? Will you do it right now? There is no greater folly that anyone can be guilty of than this – by our own free choice to remain *under the curse,* rather than to enter into the glory of becoming a child of God by just receiving Jesus Christ. No inmate of any insane asylum ever did a more insane thing than that. Will you receive Jesus Christ and become a child of God right now?

Chapter 4

How a Good Man, but an Unsaved Man, Became a Saved Man and a Child of God

Send to Joppa, and fetch Simon, whose surname is Peter; who shall speak unto thee words, whereby thou shalt be saved, thou and all thy house.
(Acts 11:13-14 ASV)

In the record of the incident from this text, we are told that Cornelius, a captain in the Roman army, and a remarkably good man in many ways, was not yet a saved man. He was told to send to Joppa for Peter the apostle; Peter would speak words to him that through hearing, believing, and acting upon, he would be saved. The life of Cornelius was already a most exemplary life in many respects, and he was a most candid, sincere, honest, and earnest seeker after the truth. Nevertheless, our text clearly teaches us he was not yet saved, although he was soon going to be saved. To my mind the story of the salvation of this man Cornelius is one of the most interesting and instructive contained in the whole Bible, not merely because he was the first gentile convert to Christianity, but also because of what he himself was.

The Character of Cornelius

Let's look closely at the character and conduct of this man Cornelius.

The inspired record declares that he *was a devout man, and one that feared God* (Acts 10:2). He was a man who lived as in the sight of God with a reverential regard for God's will and God's law. It is evident from the whole story that his devotion was genuine, for it affected his whole household. We are told that not only did he fear God, but that he also *feared God with all his house.* Furthermore, the soldiers under him and his near friends also were affected by the genuineness of his pious regard for the Deity (Acts 10:2, 7, 24). It certainly speaks well for a man's devotion when his whole family participates in it, and when those who serve under him share in it. I know few religious people whose families take much stock in their religion and whose employees consider it at all. But so genuine was the regard for God of Cornelius that his whole family shared in it and even his soldiers were affected by it.

Cornelius was not in a position that encouraged religious piety. Many have told me that it is impossible to be truly religious in our own army, but it was certainly very difficult in the old Roman army. But it was in this place of extreme difficulty that we see Cornelius maintaining his devotion at a very high level. Truly, there is no position in life where it is impossible to serve God. Someone (George C. Grubb) has said, "Have you never noticed that God's most brilliant saints have been placed in positions of peculiar difficulty?" And he cites as illustrations of this the case of Joseph in the awful court of Pharaoh, and Daniel in the depraved court of Nebuchadnezzar. He might have added Elijah in the vile court of Ahab and John the Baptist in the licentious and bloody court of Herod, and many others. No, my friend, whoever you may be who is making the excuse, "I cannot serve God in my position," that is not true. If you cannot serve God in any other way in that position, you can serve Him by giving up your position.

But Cornelius was not only a devout man toward God, he was also righteous toward men. This we are told in Acts 10:22. This was the testimony regarding him by those who went to Peter. I am sorry to say that devoutness toward God is not always accompanied by righteousness toward men. Of course, a faith in God and love for God that does not lead to honesty in dealing with men and love toward men is not an intelligent and genuine faith, but there is much of that sort of "faith in God" in the world today. There is much that passes for devotion that is not accompanied by righteousness in private, domestic, business, and political life. I have known men of most demonstrative devotedness who were utterly unreliable in business. Now I do not believe these men are all conscious hypocrites, but they certainly have a devotedness which is of no value in the sight of God. But Cornelius was a man who was righteous toward men as well as devout toward God. That is a most happy combination. I wish we had more men of that type here in Los Angeles.

In the third place, Cornelius was an exceptionally and notably generous man. God's own record concerning him is that he *gave much alms to the people* (Acts 10:2). So notable was the generosity of Cornelius's gifts to the poor that God took notice of them and kept a record of them. He even went so far as to send an angel down to say to Cornelius, *Thine alms are gone up for a memorial before God* (Acts 10:4 ASV). That is to say, they had gone up to be remembered by God. If the only memorial that some professing Christians have tonight to get into heaven are your alms to the poor, I am afraid that it will be of such small dimensions that you will have a hard time finding it when you get there. All that a good many people give to the poor is their cast-off clothing that they would not wear anymore anyhow. Not so with Cornelius, for he *gave much alms to the people.*

But even this is not all; Cornelius was a man of prayer. We are told that he *prayed to God always* (Acts 10:2 ASV). Though he was not a Jew by birth, he had become convinced of the truth of the Jewish religion and observed the regular Jewish hours of prayer. We find him praying *about the ninth hour of the day,* which was three o'clock in the afternoon, the Jewish hour of afternoon sacrifice and prayer. And furthermore, as already noted, we are told that he *prayed to God always.* He was a man who was constantly in prayer to God. He no longer worshipped or prayed to Jupiter or Juno or Venus or any of the false gods of the religion in which he was born and brought up, but to the only true God. He was a man who was constantly in prayer to God. Remember, Cornelius was not yet a Christian, but what an example he sets in this matter of prayer to many who profess to believe in Christ Jesus today. I wonder how much time the average Christian in this audience tonight, Protestant or Roman Catholic, spends in prayer daily. About the only time some Roman Catholics pray is when the priest appoints them so many Pater Nosters or Ave Marias as a penance; about the only praying a good many Protestants do is four or five minutes at bedtime. But this captain in the Roman army, just emerging from the darkness of heathenism, was a man of constant prayer, and his prayers as well as his alms had gone up as a memorial before God (Acts 10:4).

In addition to all these things, Cornelius was an eager seeker after more light. When he heard that in another city there was a man who had more truth than he had, he immediately sent for him (Acts 10:7-8, 33), and in addition to that, he *called together his kinsmen and his near friends* to hear this new truth (Acts 10:24 ASV). All the truth that there was he wanted for himself, and not only for himself but for his friends also, and he wished it at once. How unlike Cornelius are many today who call themselves honest seekers after truth but studiously avoid those who are likely to give them the truth. And if they happen to meet them, they dodge and quibble and resort to all sorts of distractions to escape from letting the light into their hearts. Many a man today calls himself a truth seeker but goes and listens to some palpable pettifogger (unethical lawyer) such as Colonel Ingersoll.[1] Cornelius was not that kind of truth seeker but was an honest and genuine one who really wanted to know the truth; he was ready to immediately obey it when he found it. Cornelius was not yet a Christian, but he was not of that type of non-Christians who are ready to listen to all sorts of disingenuous reasonings and foolish imaginations that seem to discredit Christianity. He was indeed a sincere seeker after truth.

At the very time that directions came to him from God to send to Joppa for Simon Peter, who would tell him the saving truth, he was in prayer for more light. That is evident from Acts 10:31-32, where we read that the angel said to him, *Cornelius, thy prayer is heard. . . . Send therefore to Joppa, and call unto thee Simon, whose surname is Peter.* So it is evident that the prayer that he was offering and that was heard was a prayer for light, a prayer for the truth. Every honest seeker after light will pray for it.

I would like to ask any skeptic present here tonight, "Have you ever honestly asked God to show you the light? Have you ever honestly asked God to show you if Jesus Christ was His Son or not? Have you promised Him that if He would show you that Jesus was the Son of God, you would accept Him as your Savior and confess Him as such before the world?"

Cornelius was ready to obey the truth when he found it,

---

1   Colonel Robert G. Ingersoll was an American lawyer, writer, and orator who defended agnosticism.

whatever it might require of him. This is evident from his question when God's messenger appeared. He was badly frightened, but he stood up like the obedient soldier that he was and said, *What is it, Lord?* (Acts 10:4). In other words, "Lord, give the command and I will obey it." His readiness to obey the truth is also proven by his prompt obedience to the gospel when it was declared to him (Acts 10:43-48).

Taken all together, this man Cornelius was a man of singularly lofty character. He was devout toward God, righteous toward men, and generous to the poor. He was a prayerful man and an eager seeker after truth, who was ready to obey the truth when he found it, whatever it might require. And yet with all this, the inspired record tells us Cornelius was not as yet "saved"; he still needed salvation. The word that God spoke to him was, *Send to Joppa, and fetch Simon, whose surname is Peter; who shall speak unto thee words, whereby thou shalt be saved* (Acts 11:13-14). It is clear, then, that he was not yet saved.

How many there are in this audience tonight who are trusting for salvation in just such things as Cornelius already had, and think they are saved because they have some or all of these things, though they certainly have them in much less measure than Cornelius had. Many men have told me they expected to be saved because they were religious or righteous in their daily life in their dealings with men or their generosity to the poor, or they prayed a good deal, or because they were honest seekers after the truth. Behold Cornelius! He was all these and more, and yet God declares that he was not yet saved. If any man could be saved by character, certainly Cornelius could, but he was unsaved. That fact shows the utter folly of this modern nonsensical talk about "salvation by character." Cornelius still needed something

> If any man could be saved by character, certainly Cornelius could, but he was unsaved.

that was absolutely necessary before he could be a saved man. I am glad to tell you he found it.

Every man who is as sincere a seeker after truth as Cornelius was and as ready to obey it when he finds it will certainly find it. The Lord Jesus Himself says, *If any man will do his will* [that is, God's will], *he shall know of the doctrine, whether it be of God, or whether I speak of myself* (John 7:17 AKJV). It is certain that any man who sincerely desires to know the truth and is ready to obey it when he finds it will find it and accept it as it is in Jesus and thereby be saved, but he is not actually saved until he does know this truth and receives it and acts upon it. These things, which Cornelius had, did not save him, but they prepared him to find and receive the truth as it is in Christ Jesus and thereby to be saved.

How Cornelius Found Salvation, Not Only a Good Man but Also a Saved Man

Now let's look at how Cornelius found salvation and became not only a good man, but also a saved man and a child of God.

Cornelius prayed for light. This appears from God saying to him, *Thy prayer is heard. Send to Joppa, and fetch Simon, whose surname is Peter; who shall speak unto thee words, whereby thou shalt be saved* (Acts 10:31; 11:13-14). Cornelius felt that he did not have the whole truth. He knew that he didn't have peace. He knew that for all his excellencies of character, he was a sinner and needed pardon; he sought from God to find out where pardon could be found. Whoever desires to know the truth and whoever desires pardon, let him seek light from God, and let him ask God to point him to the One in whom pardon is to be found. That prayer will not save him, but it will lead him to the One who will save him.

I could stand here by the hour and give you illustrations of men and women whom I have known from almost every rank of society, who were in sincere doubt as to whether Jesus Christ was the Son of God and whether He could and would save, but they sought light from God and got it. They were thus brought to an intelligent faith in Jesus Christ as the Son of God and as their own personal crucified and risen Savior; they thereby found salvation.

Cornelius obeyed, step by step, the light as God gave him to see it. There are some who will not take one single step until God shows them the whole way. Such people never find the way. But if we are ready to take a step at a time as God indicates it to us, God will lead us on into the perfect day. For example, I know men who will not take the steps in the truth, which they acknowledge are perfectly clear, because they do not yet understand all the mysteries concerning future punishment, and God's purposes concerning the heathen, and predestination, and other questions like that. Cornelius was not like that. Cornelius only asked to see a step at a time; as soon as he saw the next step, he took it, and therefore he was soon out in the clear daylight. So will it be with you if you will follow Cornelius's example. The very first step that Cornelius was told to take was a test of faith; he was told to send for an unknown Jew in the home of a tanner, and this Jew would show him the way of life. How absurd that must have looked! Weren't the Jews in subjection to the Romans? And wasn't Rome the land of culture and Judea the land of superstition? And wasn't this particular Jew an uneducated man? Should he, a cultured Roman officer, send for an ignorant Jew to teach him? But Cornelius knew God had commanded it, so he raised no objections and asked no questions, but obeyed orders and did exactly as he was told.

Ah, how many of us refuse to obey God's orders because we are so filled with the conceit of our own culture and our own superior position; therefore, we never get out of the fog and darkness into which our self-sufficiency has plunged us. We proudly refuse to obey God because we cannot understand the reasonableness of His commands, so we miss the path of unquestioning obedience to God that would lead us into the glorious light of the Son of God.

Cornelius's third step toward salvation was that he heard the simple gospel of Christ crucified, Christ risen again, and Christ's provision for remission of sins to be obtained through simple faith in this crucified, risen Christ, the Lord of all. The sermon that Cornelius heard was very short, and it was the first Christian sermon he had ever heard. He may have heard before that there was such a person as Jesus, but he knew little or nothing about Him. Peter simply told him a few fundamental facts about Jesus: how God preached good tidings of peace by Him, how Jesus Christ was Lord of all, how God anointed Him with the Holy Spirit and with power, and how He went about doing good, and healing all that were oppressed by the devil; for God was with him. Peter told him how he was a witness of all things which Jesus of Nazareth did, and then he told him how they slew Him and hanged him on a tree. Then he told him how on the third day God raised him up and how he was an eyewitness of His appearances in His body after His resurrection. He ate and drank with Jesus after He arose from the dead; then Peter told Cornelius how this Jesus was *ordained of God to be the Judge of the living and the dead* and how *to him bear all the prophets witness, that through his name every one that believeth on him shall receive remission of sins* (Acts 10:42-43 ASV).

That was all that Peter told him, and that was enough. Cornelius believed it and was instantly saved. All that Cornelius heard you have heard time and again, and as far as hearing and knowing the truth are concerned, you have heard enough and already know enough to be saved.

Then Cornelius took the decisive step. He believed in Jesus

Christ, right there and then; he was saved at once. Will you take the same decisive step tonight, the simple step of believing on Christ Jesus, of whom it is conclusively proven that He died on the cross and thus made full atonement for sin? He secured pardon for all who would believe on Him, and He arose again and therefore has power to keep from the power of sin all those who put their trust in Him (Hebrews 7:25). Will you take that step?

As good and exemplary as Cornelius was, he was saved in the same way that the coarse, brutal, prayerless, and godless Philippian jailer in the sixteenth chapter of the Acts of the Apostles was saved, that is, by simple faith in Jesus Christ for the pardon of sin and for deliverance from sin's power.

When Peter spoke of the forgiveness of sins, Cornelius knew he needed it. If you have not already received Jesus Christ as your own personal Savior, you need to do so tonight. When Peter said, *Every one that believeth on him shall receive remission of sins,* Cornelius said to himself, "That means me," and he believed right then and there, and received remission of sins right then and there. Anyone tonight can receive remission of sins exactly the same way that Cornelius did and just as quickly as Cornelius did. The word preached to Cornelius says, *Through his name every one that believeth on him shall receive remission of sins.* Even though you are as good as Cornelius, you need pardon; even though you are as vile as the vilest, you can have it. *Every one that believeth on him shall receive remission of sins.*

> Even though you are as good as Cornelius, you need pardon; even though you are as vile as the vilest, you can have it.

Let me call your attention to one more thing. The Holy Spirit came upon Cornelius right then in testimony to the fact that God had accepted him, and he began to *magnify God* in the power of the Holy Spirit. And so not only pardon, but also the Holy Spirit's power is for everyone tonight who will believe on the Lord Jesus.

There is still one more thing that Cornelius did that needs to be carefully noted: Cornelius openly confessed his acceptance of Jesus Christ and his identification with Him in baptism. He was already saved. He already had God's seal of acceptance – the definite, conscious work of the Holy Spirit – but that did not make him say, "There is no need that I be baptized. I have everything already." No, rather it made him say, "I want to obey God and confess my faith in Jesus Christ in God's appointed way by baptism." The faith in Jesus Christ that Cornelius had was real, saving faith, and saving faith always leads to obedience. The Christ in whom Cornelius believed as Savior and Lord had commanded baptism, so he was baptized immediately. And if you really believe in Jesus Christ, you will desire to obey Christ in everything. If you have not been baptized already, you will desire to be baptized. And even if you have been baptized already, you will do that for which baptism is an outward sign – make an open confession of your acceptance of Jesus Christ as your crucified, dead, buried, and risen Lord and Savior.

Salvation is open to everyone tonight. It cannot be obtained by any amount of piety toward God, righteousness toward man, generosity in giving, earnestness in praying, or sincerity in the search for the truth. By everyone, good and bad, moral and immoral, highly respected and utterly despised, it must be obtained in the same way – by a simple faith in Christ Jesus, who died for us on the cross of Calvary and rose again – faith in Him as your Savior and your Lord. Who will thus put their faith in Him tonight?

Chapter 5

Saved by Calling Out

Whosoever shall call upon the name of the Lord shall be saved. (Romans 10:13)

No man has any excuse for not knowing the way of salvation, for the Bible makes it as plain as day. No man has any excuse for not taking the way of salvation, for God has made that way so simple and so open to everybody that *whosoever will may come.* Many years ago, I took a pedestrian tour with a friend through the Saxon Switzerland National Park in Saxony, Germany. One day we struck off from the main road and went across country on a bypath. We suddenly came upon a signboard with a crown on it and the information that the road was for the king and only for the king; common mortals were not allowed that way. But God's way of salvation is open to all: *Whosoever shall call upon the name of the Lord shall be saved.*

The way of salvation is stated in the Bible in a variety of forms so that everybody can understand it. In one place we are told that we are saved by just coming to Jesus. He Himself says, *Come unto me, all ye that labor and are heavy laden, and I will give you rest* (Matthew 11:28). He also says, *Him that cometh to me I will in no wise cast out* (John 6:37).

Later we are told that we are saved by just believing on the Lord Jesus. The Philippian jailer had cried, *Sirs, what must I do to be saved?* Paul replied, *Believe on the Lord Jesus, and thou shalt be saved* (Acts 16:31 ASV).

In another place we are told that we are saved by just receiving (or taking) the Lord Jesus. John's words are, *As many as received him, to them gave he the right to become children of God, even to them that believe on his name* (John 1:12 ASV). We are also told that we are saved by just looking to Jesus Christ. The Lord says, *Look unto me, and be ye saved* (Isaiah 45:22).

But to my mind, the simplest statement of all is that of our text, where we are told that we are saved by just calling on the name of the Lord: *Whosoever shall call upon the name of the Lord shall be saved* (Romans 10:13). Saved simply by a cry, a cry to the Lord Jesus, for that Jesus is the Lord in this passage, which is evident from the ninth verse of the same chapter, where we are told that *if thou shalt confess with thy mouth Jesus as Lord, and shalt believe in thy heart that God raised him from the dead, thou shalt be saved* (Romans 10:9 ASV).

The statement of the way of salvation contained in our text is so simple that some stumble at its very simplicity. "Oh," they say, "God can't mean that all I have to do to be saved is just to cry to the Lord Jesus, simply call upon the name of the Lord." But that is what God says; don't you think that God knows enough to say exactly what He means?

Don't you think that God knows enough to say exactly what He means?

In order for there to be no possible doubt that He meant just what He said, God has put this statement in three different places in the Bible. You will find it first of all way back in the Old Testament in Joel 2:32 (ASV), where we read, *Whosoever shall call on the name of Jehovah shall be delivered.* Then Peter repeated the statement on the day of Pentecost, saying, *And it shall be, that whosoever shall call on the name of the Lord shall be saved* (Acts 2:21 ASV). Paul repeats it again in our text: *Whosoever shall call upon the name of the Lord shall be saved* (Romans 10:13). It is very seldom that you can find the very same statement made three different times in the Word of God. Can you doubt a statement God takes pains to repeat three times?

And that is not all. Besides this, God gives us a number of examples in the Bible of men who were saved just this way, by a cry, by calling to the Lord Jesus for deliverance. Peter is as good an example as any. Peter was sinking in the Sea of Galilee as he tried to walk across the waves to meet Jesus, and in his terror he just cried to Jesus as he was going down, *Lord, save me. And immediately Jesus stretched forth his hand, and took hold of him* (Matthew 14:30-31 ASV). Saved just by a cry, and anyone who is sinking in a sea of sin can be saved in precisely the same way. Jesus is ready to take hold of you tonight if you only cry to Him, and if He takes hold of you, your rescue is sure.

There are three important questions suggested by our text:

1. What is the salvation promised?

2. How can we get this salvation?

3. Who can have this salvation?

What Is the Salvation Promised?

The first question is, What is the salvation promised? The answer to this question is very plain and very easily understood. Listen to the text again: *Whosoever shall call upon the name of the Lord shall be saved.* Saved from what? If you will go back to the preceding chapters of this same book from which our text is taken, you will get your answer.

First of all, the one who calls on the name of the Lord will be saved from the guilt of sin. This comes from the third chapter:

For all have sinned, and fall short of the glory of God; being justified freely by his grace through the redemption that is in Christ Jesus: whom God set forth to be a propitiation, through faith, in his blood, to show his righteousness because of the passing over of the sins done aforetime in the forbearance of God; for the showing, I say, of his righteousness at this present season: that he might himself be just, and the justifier of him that hath faith in Jesus (Romans 3:23-26 ASV).

We see from these verses that the one who calls on the Lord Jesus gets for himself justification, deliverance from condemnation, and salvation from the guilt of sin that the Lord Jesus made possible for us by dying as a propitiation for our sins on the cross. The same thought of salvation is found in Galatians: *For as many as are of the works of the law are under a curse: for it is written, Cursed is every one who continueth not in all things that are written in the book of the law, to do them. Christ redeemed us from the curse of the law, having become a curse for us; for it is written, Cursed is every one that hangeth on a tree* (Galatians 3:10, 13 ASV).

Christ took our place on the cross of Calvary, and the moment we believe on Him, we step into His place of perfect acceptance before God. Not only is every one of our sins blotted out, but His perfect righteousness is also put to our account, and the simplest and most practical way of expressing our faith in Him is by just calling upon Him. Crying unto Him for pardon is the proof that we believe on Him; and so in crying unto Him, we are thereby justified. We are also told this in the very next verse to our text: *How then shall they call on him in whom they have not believed?* (Romans 10:14). The moment we thus call upon the Lord Jesus, all our sins are blotted out;

> **Christ took our place on the cross of Calvary, and the moment we believe on Him, we step into His place of perfect acceptance before God.**

God Himself erases everything He has in His books against us and puts the perfect righteousness and acceptability of Christ Jesus to our account.

But that is not all. In the second place, the one who calls on the name of the Lord Jesus gets salvation from the power of sin. This we see in Romans 6:16 (ASV): *Know ye not, that to whom ye present yourselves as servants unto obedience, his servants ye are whom ye obey; whether of sin unto death, or of obedience unto righteousness?* The word translated *servants* in this verse means literally "slaves." Every sinner is a slave of the sin to which he has yielded obedience, but the moment he calls upon the Lord Jesus, he gets deliverance from this bondage, just as the demoniac who cried to the Lord got deliverance from his bondage to the demon, and the leper who cried to the Lord got deliverance from his leprosy. The Lord Jesus Himself puts it this way in John 8:36 (ASV): *If therefore the Son shall make you free, ye shall be free indeed.*

Our Lord Jesus not only died for us, and thus made salvation from the guilt of sin possible, but He also rose again and made salvation from the power of sin possible for us. This thought of the saving power of the risen Lord Jesus comes in the same chapter from which our text is taken: *Because if thou shalt confess with thy mouth Jesus as Lord, and shalt believe in thy heart that God raised him from the dead, thou shalt be saved: for with the heart man believeth unto righteousness, and with the mouth confession is made unto salvation* (Romans 10:9-10 ASV).

In the third place, the one who calls on the name of the Lord also gets salvation from the penalty of sin. We see this in Romans 6:23 (ASV): *For the wages of sin is death, but the free gift of God is eternal life in Christ Jesus our Lord.* The one who calls upon the name of the Lord – and the context shows that the *Lord* here is the Lord Jesus – the one who cries unto Jesus as his divine Lord for deliverance gets deliverance from the death that is the penalty of sin. We see this *death* in its full outworking and significance in Revelation 21:8 (AKJV): *The fearful, and unbelieving, and the abominable, and murderers, and whoremongers, and sorcerers, and idolaters, and all liars, shall have their part in the lake which burneth with fire and brimstone: which is the second death.*

Hell, in spite of all its awful and everlasting shame and pain, has no terrors whatever for the one who calls upon the name of the Lord Jesus, for he knows on the authority of God's own sure word that no matter how great a sinner he may have been, he has no part in the eternal shame and torment of hell.

To sum it all up: salvation from the guilt of sin, salvation from the power of sin, and salvation from the eternal penalty of sin is the salvation one gets by just calling on the Lord Jesus for such salvation. That certainly is a glorious salvation. But even that is not all, for we are not only saved *from* something, but we are also saved *to* something. We are not only saved from the guilt of sin and from the power of sin and from the eternal penalty of sin, but we are also saved to liberty, to sonship of God, and to an inheritance – a joint inheritance with Jesus Christ Himself. We read this in Romans 8 (ASV): *For the law of the Spirit of life in Christ Jesus made me free from the law of sin and death* (v. 2). *For as many as are led by the Spirit of God, these are sons of God* (v. 14). *The Spirit himself beareth witness with our spirit, that we are children of God: and if children, then heirs; heirs of God, and joint-heirs with Christ* (vv. 16-17).

How Can We Get This Salvation?

Now the question arises, How can we get this salvation? The text tells us that we get this salvation by simply calling *upon the name of the Lord: Whosoever shall call upon the name of the Lord shall be saved* (Romans 10:13 ASV).

What does it mean to *call upon the name of the Lord*? It means just what it says: all any one of you has to do to be saved is to call upon the Lord Jesus to save you. This is evident from the preceding verse: *For there is no distinction between Jew and Greek: for the same Lord is Lord of all, and is rich unto all that call upon him* (Romans 10:12 ASV). Bartimaeus was blind, and he got sight by crying, *Jesus, thou son of David, have mercy on me* (Mark 10:47 ASV). The leper got cleansing by crying to the Lord Jesus, *If thou wilt, thou canst make me clean. And being moved with compassion, he [Jesus] stretched forth his hand, and touched him, and saith unto him, I will; be thou made clean* (Mark 1:40-41 ASV). The publican got pardon by just crying, *God be merciful to me a sinner* (Luke 18:13 AKJV); and so we get salvation from the guilt and the power and penalty of sin by crying to the Lord Jesus for it.

> No man is going to call upon the Lord for salvation in any real way if he does not realize that he needs to be saved.

Of course, the cry to the Lord Jesus that really gets salvation must be a real cry; it must be genuine; it must be sincere; it must be honest. I hear many call, "Lord Jesus, save me," and they do not get saved. Why? Because the cry is not real; it is not genuine; it is not sincere; it is not honest; it is not earnest.

What does a real call upon the Lord Jesus for salvation imply?
First of all, a real call upon the Lord Jesus implies a realization that we need salvation, a realization that we are sinners, and a realization that we are lost. No man is going to call upon the Lord for salvation in any real way if he does not realize that he needs to be saved. To call upon the Lord Jesus to save you when you do not know you are lost, or do not believe you are lost, is a mockery.

Many people, however, call upon the Lord Jesus today

without any genuine realization that they are lost. Many cry, "Lord Jesus, save me." But if you should ask them, "Do you really believe you are lost? Do you really believe you are a guilty sinner before a holy God? Do you really believe you are under the curse of the law of God which you have broken? Do you realize you are a slave to sin? Do you realize you are sinking down into an everlasting hell? Do you believe that you are a poor, vile, miserable, worthless, hell-deserving sinner?" they would likely flare up and say, "I am nothing of the kind; I am just as good as you are. I don't believe that old worn-out superstition about human depravity and everlasting perdition and all that." Well, then, you cannot genuinely call upon the Lord Jesus to save you, and you cannot be genuinely saved. You are mocking God when you do call upon the Lord for salvation when you do not really think you are lost, hopelessly lost, without the Lord Jesus. There is no more hideous mockery than for a man who does not believe that he is lost, to call on the Lord Jesus to save him.

In the second place, a real calling upon the Lord Jesus to save implies a sincere desire for salvation. Many men call upon the Lord Jesus to save them who do not really desire to be saved; they think they do, but they don't. I have seen men kneel down and cry, "Lord Jesus, save me," and they did not want a bit to be saved. Perhaps they thought they did. They wished to be saved from hell, but that is not the essential point of salvation. Everybody wants to be saved from hell. Even the foulest infidels want to be saved from hell. Nobody wants to spend eternity in hell. But being saved from hell is not the essential thing in real salvation, and desiring merely to be saved from hell is not really desiring to be saved. Many desire to be saved from the trouble and misery that sin has gotten them into. There is not a person in the county jail that does not want to get out. But desiring to be saved from the consequences of sin is not a true desire for salvation.

A true desire for salvation is a desire for salvation from sin itself; that is the most important thing about it. The man who does not desire to give up all sin – not merely the sins that are getting him into trouble – does not really desire to be saved, and a call of such a person upon the Lord Jesus is a mockery and will do him no more good than whistling, "I want to be an angel."

> A true desire for salvation is a desire for salvation from sin itself; that is the most important thing about it.

This is why the cries of many of you for salvation do no good whatever. You don't really wish to be saved from sin, but merely from the unpleasant consequences of sin. A man in Chicago was once lamenting to a friend of mine that he could not be saved. My friend answered bluntly, "You don't want to be saved."

"Yes, I do," the man answered with tears.

"No, you don't," my friend insisted. Then he asked him, "Do you want to quit drinking?"

The man was silent a while and then said, "I don't know as I do."

That is the way with thousands. Others may wish to quit drinking, but there are other sins they do not wish to quit. Do you really desire to quit all sin, to quit doing anything and everything that displeases God? If you do, you have a real desire for salvation, and if you cry to the Lord Jesus He will save you. *Blessed are they,* says Jesus Christ, *that hunger and thirst after righteousness: for they shall be filled* (Matthew 5:6 ASV).

The desire for salvation must also be earnest; it must be a desire to be saved at any cost. When a man so earnestly desires salvation from the guilt, the power, and the consequences of sin that he is willing to pay any price to get it, he will get it, and not until then. God says in Jeremiah 29:13, *Ye shall seek me, and find me, when ye shall search for me with all your heart.*

In the third place, a real calling upon the name of the Lord for salvation implies a throwing away of all confidence in anyone else and in anything else and everything else as a way of salvation. The man who is trying to save himself cannot honestly call upon the Lord Jesus to save him; the man who is trusting in his own good works, his own personal piety, his own benevolence, or his turning over a new leaf or any other thing he can do, cannot truly call upon the Lord. This is the trouble with many of you; you have not reached the end of yourself and your own efforts; you still hope to do something to commend yourself to the Lord. Only the man who realizes his own helplessness, his own inability to do anything to cover his guilt or break away from sin or escape its consequences can throw himself in utter helplessness on the Lord Jesus and cry to Him to save him as poor sinking Peter cried, *Lord, save me.*

There is one more thing that an honest call upon the Lord Jesus implies, and that is faith in Him, faith in His power to save. This comes from the verse immediately following our text: *How then shall they call on him in whom they have not believed?* (Romans 10:14 ASV). If my cry to the Lord Jesus means anything, it means this: faith that Jesus can and will save me. This faith may not be very strong; it may not be very confident; it may be very weak, but there must be faith enough to call with some expectation, no matter how small, that we shall be saved. We may have to come to Jesus with just a little faith, like the man whose son was a demoniac, and he cried to Jesus, *If thou canst do any thing, have compassion on us, and help us. Jesus said unto him, If thou canst believe, all things are possible to him that believeth. And straightway the father of the child cried out, and said with tears, Lord, I believe; help thou mine unbelief. But Jesus took him by the hand, and lifted him up; and he arose* (Mark 9:22-24, 27 AKJV).

The Lord Jesus responded to his feeble faith and helped his unbelief by doing what he sought; so will He do for us if we come in that honest, earnest way, even though our faith is small. All one needs to do, then, to be saved is (1) realize his own need of salvation, (2) earnestly desire to be saved, (3) throw away all trust in anyone and anything else but Jesus, (4) believe He can and will save, and (5) call upon Him to do it. That is all – *Whosoever shall call upon the name of the Lord shall be saved* (Romans 10:13 ASV).

Who Can Have This Salvation?

Now, just a few words on who can have this salvation. The answer to this question is very plain, as it is set forth in the text: *Whosoever shall call upon the name of the Lord shall be saved* (Romans 10:13). The Greek words translated *whosoever* mean "everyone who." I sometimes wish that the verse had been translated literally and so read in this way: "Everyone who shall call upon the name of the Lord shall be saved." That surely means everybody. It means rich or poor, wise or foolish, learned or ignorant, good or bad, moral or vicious.

John Berridge once said in preaching on this text, "I would much rather it be written, 'Whosoever shall call upon the name of the Lord shall be saved,' than 'If John Berridge shall call on the name of the Lord, John Berridge shall be saved,' because how do I know but that there might be another John Berridge in the world to whom these words were addressed? But when I read, *Whosoever shall call upon the name of the Lord shall be saved,* I know I must be included."

Yes, thank God, that is the way it reads: *Whosoever* [or everyone who] *shall call upon the name of the Lord shall be saved.* The good man can get salvation in this way and in no other way, and the bad man can get salvation in this way and in no other way. All any man needs to know in order to be saved is just enough to call on the name of the Lord Jesus. The skeptic may be saved this way. He may have many doubts, but if he believes he is lost, if he honestly desires to be saved, if he throws away confidence in everyone and everything else and has enough faith to call on the Lord Jesus, even though it be almost in despair, he can put this promise to a practical test: *Whosoever shall call upon the name of the Lord shall be saved.*

> **All any man needs to know in order to be saved is just enough to call on the name of the Lord Jesus.**

Many are saying, "I have sinned away the day of grace, and therefore I cannot be saved." But God says, *Whosoever shall call upon the name of the Lord shall be saved.* All that you, as well as anybody else, has to do then is just to call. Just call.

Another says, "I have committed the unpardonable sin; therefore there is no hope for me." But God says, *Whosoever shall call upon the name of the Lord shall be saved.* Just call, then.

Another says, "But my sins have been so many and so black that there is no hope for me." But God says, *Whosoever shall call upon the name of the Lord shall be saved.* Just call, then.

Another says, "But I have had so much light and sinned against it; there certainly can be no hope for me." But God says, *Whosoever shall call upon the name of the Lord shall be saved.* Just call, then.

But another says, "I have no feeling; my heart is as hard as a stone. Surely there is no hope for me." But God says, *Whosoever shall call upon the name of the Lord shall be saved.* Just call, then.

But another says, "I am sure I cannot hold out even if I start, so there is no hope for me." But God says, *Whosoever shall call upon the name of the Lord shall be saved.* Just call, then.

Whosoever, Whosoever, Whosoever. This wonderful text sweeps away all our excuses. It throws the door wide open for anyone to enter tonight who has any real desire to be saved. Some old theologian pictured Peter preaching on the day of Pentecost:

A man pushed his way through the crowd and said, "Peter, do you think there is hope for me? I am the man who made that crown of thorns and placed them on Christ's brow. Do you think He will save me?"

"Yes," said Peter. *"Whosoever shall call upon the name of the Lord shall be saved,* and you are a whosoever; if you call, he will hear your cry. He will answer your prayer and save you."

Another man pushed his way up and said, "Peter, I am the man who took the reed out of his hand and drove it upon that cruel crown of thorns, sending it into his brow. Do you think he will save me?"

"Yes," said Peter. *"Whosoever shall call upon the name of the Lord shall be saved.* You are a whosoever, and if you call upon the name of the Lord, you shall be saved."

Another man, elbowing his way through the crowd, pushed up to Peter and said, "I am the Roman soldier who took the spear and thrust it into his heart and out came blood and water. Do you think there is hope for me?"

"Yes," said Peter, "there is a nearer way of reaching his heart than that: *Whosoever shall call upon the name of the Lord shall be saved"* (Pith & Point in Story and Saying).

Yes, it is true, Whosoever, Whosoever, *Whosoever shall call upon the name of the Lord shall be saved.* Who will call tonight? Who will awaken to the fact that you need salvation, that you are a poor, vile, lost, worthless, miserable, hell-deserving sinner? Who will let God put into his heart a real desire to be saved tonight, to be saved not merely from the unpleasant consequences of sin but also to be saved from sin itself? Who will right now throw away all confidence in anyone else or in anything else and everything else as a way of salvation, except the crucified and risen Son of God? Who will put faith enough in Jesus Christ tonight and Jesus Christ's ability to save him? Who will just call upon Him, even though it is with very feeble expectation of being heard? Salvation stands waiting at the door to enter the heart and life of every unsaved man, woman, and child here tonight. All you have to do to open the door wide for salvation is just to *call upon the name of the Lord* Jesus. Will you do it right now?

Chapter 6

How to Be Unspeakably Happy Under All Circumstances

Whom not having seen ye love; on whom, though now ye see him not, yet believing, ye rejoice greatly with joy unspeakable and full of glory. (1 Peter 1:8 ASV)

I have here a beautiful text, a text that you all know, but I wonder how many of you have ever pondered it enough to take in all its wonderful wealth of meaning.

A young woman in England many years ago always wore a golden locket that she would not allow anyone to open or look into; everyone thought there must be some romance connected with that locket and that in that locket must be the picture of the one she loved. The young woman died at an early age, and after her death the locket was opened, everyone wondering whose face they would find within. And in the locket was simply a little slip of paper with these words written upon it: *Whom having not seen, I love.* Her Lord Jesus was the only lover she knew and the only lover she longed for, and she had gone to be with Him, the one object of her whole heart's devotion, the unseen but beloved Savior.

But I wish to call your particular attention to the last part of the verse: *On whom, though now ye see him not, yet believing, ye rejoice greatly with joy unspeakable and full of glory.*

This text informs us (and many of us do not need to be informed of it, for we know it by blessed experience) that the one who really believes on Jesus Christ, our unseen but ever-living Lord and Savior, rejoices with *joy unspeakable and full of glory.* The Greek word translated *joy* is a very strong word, describing extreme joy or exultant joy. The word *unspeakable* declares that this exultant joy is of such a character that we cannot possibly explain it to others. Everyone who really believes on the Lord Jesus does rejoice with an exultant joy that is beyond all description. And those who do truly believe on the Lord Jesus Christ are the only ones who do thus rejoice. Others may have a certain amount of joy, a certain measure of gladness, but the only people who really know *joy unspeakable and full of glory* are those who really believe on Jesus Christ.

Who is there among us who does not wish to be happy? Happiness is the one thing all men are seeking. One man seeks it in one way, and another man seeks it in another way, but all men are in pursuit of happiness. Even the man who is happy only when he is miserable is seeking happiness in this strange way of cultivating a delightful melancholy by always looking on the dark side of things. One man seeks money because he thinks that money will make him happy. Another man seeks worldly pleasure because he thinks that worldly pleasure will make him happy. Still another seeks learning, the knowledge of science, philosophy, history, or literature because he thinks that learning brings the true joy; but they are all in pursuit of the one thing – happiness.

The vast majority of men who seek happiness do not find it. You may say what you please, but for the majority of men, this is an unhappy world. I go into the houses of the poor, and I do not find many happy people there. I go into the homes of the rich, and I do not find many happy people there either. Study the faces of the people you meet in cars, on the street, at entertainments, or anywhere else; how many really radiant faces do you see? When you do see one, it is so exceptional that you note it at once. But there is a way, a very simple way, a very sure way, and a way that is open to all not only to find happiness but also to be unspeakably happy. Our text tells us what that way is. *On whom, though now ye see him not, yet believing, ye rejoice greatly with joy unspeakable and full of glory.*

This statement of Peter's is true. How do I know it is true? In the first place, I know it is true because the Word of God says so. Whatever this Book says is true. In the second place, I know it is true because I have put the matter to the test of personal experiment and found it true. A good many people say, "I do not believe the Bible." Well, I do. I believe the Bible for a good many sufficient reasons, but there is one reason why I believe the Bible that I wish to mention now: I believe the Bible because I have personally tested scores and scores of its most astonishing and apparently most incredible statements and found every one of them true in my own experience.

> I know it is true because the Word of God says so. Whatever this Book says is true.

What if I knew a man who made many statements that I could test for myself, some of them apparently incredible, and I tested these statements one after another through a long period of years and found every one of them true. What if not one single statement failed; don't you think that I would believe that man after a while? Well, that is just my experience with the Bible, and I believe it. I would be a fool if I did not. The statement of the text is one of those that I have tested, and I have found it true.

I was not always happy. Indeed, I was once unspeakably miserable. I had sought happiness very earnestly. I had sought happiness in gaiety and sin, and I found not joy but wretchedness. In my pursuit of happiness, I had tried study – the study of languages, science, philosophy, and literature, but I did not find happiness in these things. At last I turned to Jesus Christ and believed on Him, and I found not merely happiness but also something better – joy, *joy unspeakable and full of glory.* Whatever heaven may be or may not be, I know that on this earth the one who believes on Jesus Christ, the one who puts himself in Christ's hands to be led, taught, guided, and strengthened, who puts himself in the hands of Jesus Christ to do all He will with him – I know that such a person finds *joy unspeakable and full of glory.*

Why Those Who Believe in Jesus Christ Have Joy Unspeakable and Full of Glory

First of all, those who believe on Jesus Christ have *joy unspeakable and full of glory* because they know that their sins are all forgiven. There is not one single, slightest cloud between you and God. It is amazing to know that no matter how many or how great your sins may have been, they are all blotted out, and God has put them all behind His back where no one can ever get at them. It is marvelous to know that God sunk all your sins in the depths of the sea from which they can never be raised; they are all gone.

A little boy once asked his mother, "Mother, where are our sins after they are blotted out?"

His mother replied, "My boy, where are those figures that were on your slate yesterday?"

He answered, "I rubbed them out."

Then she asked, "Where are they now?"

He replied, "They are nowhere."

"Well," she said, "that is just so with your sins when God has blotted them out. They are nowhere. They have ceased to be."

Oh friends, what a joy it is to know that there is not one single, smallest cloud between you and the Holy God whom we call Father and who rules this universe. Suppose that you had violated the laws of the nation and had been committed to prison on a life sentence, and a pardon was offered to you. Don't you think you would be happy? But that is nothing compared with the joy of knowing that your every sin is blotted out.

Some years ago, Governor Stuart of Pennsylvania decided to pardon one of the prisoners in the Pennsylvania state prison, so he sent for Mr. Moody and said to him, "I have decided to pardon one of the prisoners in our state's prison, and I want you to go and take the pardon to him. You can preach to the prisoners while you are doing it if you want to."

So Mr. Moody went, carrying the pardon with him, and before he began to preach, he said, "I have a pardon for one of you men that the governor has sent with me." He did not intend to tell who was pardoned until the sermon was over, but as he looked at his audience and saw how anxious they all were, how eager they were, how an agony of suspense was in their faces, Mr. Moody thought, "This will never do. I can't keep **Every true Christian knows that every one of his sins is forgiven.** these men in this suspense." So he said, "I will tell you now who the man is," and he read his name from the pardon.

Don't you think that was a glad moment for that one man out of those hundreds of prisoners, a glad moment for the one man who had the governor's pardon, and who could walk out of prison a free man? Ah, but that is nothing when compared to knowing that the eternal God has eternally pardoned your sins. Every true Christian knows that every one of his sins is forgiven. How does he know? Because the Bible says so in many places. It says in Acts 13:39 (ASV), *By him every one that believeth is justified from all things.* So we know it because God says so. But no one but the believer on Jesus Christ knows that his sins are all forgiven. If anyone who is not a believer on Jesus Christ says, "I know my sins are all forgiven," he says what is not true. They don't know it, and cannot know it, for it is not a fact; but a Christian knows it because the Word of God says so.

The Christian knows his sins are forgiven for another reason: that is, because the Holy Spirit bears witness in his heart to the fact. One day when the apostle Peter was preaching to Cornelius, the Roman officer, and to his household, he said, *To him bear all the prophets witness, that through his name every one that believeth on him shall receive remission of sins* (Acts 10:43 ASV), and everyone in his audience believed it. The Spirit of God descended right then and there and filled their hearts with the knowledge of sins forgiven, and they began to magnify God with exultant hearts and exultant voices. I tell you that was a joyful meeting.

A king, a great king, once wrote one of the greatest songs that was ever written. That song has lasted through the ages. It has been sung and is still being sung by thousands. It has been sung by millions, and though it was written many centuries ago, it is just as sweet today as the day the king wrote it. The man who wrote this song was a great king, the greatest king of his day; he was also one of the greatest generals of his day, one of the greatest generals of any day. He had great armies, the all-conquering armies of the day. He had a magnificent palace. I don't suppose that any other earthly king was ever so beloved as he was. His song was about joy and about happiness. He does not say in that song, "How happy is the man who is a great king," or "How happy is the man who is a great general." What does he say? "Oh, the happinesses of the man whose transgression is forgiven, whose sin is covered" (Psalm 32:1, translated literally from the Hebrew).

There is no happiness like the joy of knowing your sins are all forgiven. Oh, what a joy thrills the heart when a man knows that his sins are fully, freely, and forever forgiven. That is one reason why the one who believes on Jesus Christ is unspeakably happy, and you can have that unspeakable happiness today. I do not care how black your life may have

There is no happiness like the joy of knowing your sins are all forgiven.

been in the past; I do not care how far you may have wandered from God; I do not care how old you may have grown in sin. If you take Jesus Christ today for your Savior and your Lord and believe on Him, your every sin will be blotted out, and it will be your privilege to know it.

In the second place, those who believe on Jesus Christ *rejoice greatly with joy unspeakable and full of glory* because they are free from the most grinding and crushing of all forms of slavery, the slavery of sin. There is many a slave in this audience tonight. Some of you are slaves of strong drink. Some of you men and some of you women are slaves of drink. You know you are slaves of drink. Some of you are slaves of drugs. Some of you are slaves of an ungovernable temper. Some of you are slaves of impure acts or impure thoughts. Some of you are slaves of other sins. The grossest, vilest, most degrading slavery in the universe is the slavery of sin. Yes, many of you here tonight are slaves.

But the Lord Jesus says, *If ye continue in my word, then are ye my disciples indeed; and ye shall know the truth, and the truth shall make you free* (John 8:31-32 AKJV). Later He says, *If the Son therefore shall make you free, ye shall be free indeed* (John 8:36 AKJV). There is not a slave in this building tonight who cannot have his bonds broken in a moment – yes, in a moment, by the mighty Son of God, if he will only believe on Him and trust Him to do it. How many a man and how many a woman I have known who were once slaves of sin in its most degrading and hopeless forms, who are now free.

One of the dearest and most honored and most useful friends I ever had was Sam Hadley of New York City. Sam Hadley was once hopelessly enslaved by sin. Strong drink had utterly mastered him and undermined his character. Because he had committed 138 forgeries, he was being sought by the police. One night, after spending the previous horrible night locked up in a New York jail with delirium tremens, he cried to Jesus to save him while in a mission meeting a few blocks away. Jesus saved him right then and there, and I have often heard him say that never from that night forward has he ever had the slightest desire for that which had enslaved him more than anything else, intoxicating drink. What a happy man he became! All who knew him testified that he had *joy unspeakable and full of glory*. I wish you could have looked in Sam Hadley's face and seen the joy that there was in that redeemed and radiant countenance.

But we do not need to call Sam Hadley back from heaven to testify, for there are hundreds of people right here in this building tonight who were once complete slaves but are now God's free men and free women, who could testify to the fact. That is one reason we are unspeakably happy – because we are free. How the Southern Blacks rejoiced when they came to understand they were emancipated. They shouted and sang, "Glory! Glory! Hallelujah!" Why? Because they were once slaves but now were free. No wonder we rejoice with *joy unspeakable and full of glory*, because we know that we are free and free forever.

In the third place, those who believe on Jesus Christ *rejoice greatly with joy unspeakable and full of glory* because they are delivered from all fear. There is nothing that darkens the human heart more and robs it of all joy and fills it with gloom than fear in some of its myriad forms. Those who truly believe on Jesus Christ are saved from all fear. They are delivered from all fear of misfortune; they are delivered from all fear of man; they are delivered from all fear of death; they are delivered from all fear of eternity.

Do you know, friends, that to a true believer in Jesus Christ *eternity* is one of the sweetest words in the English language? Oh, how it makes our hearts swell, that word *eternity*. But *eternity* is not a sweet word to the unsaved. Write these words, *Where will you spend eternity?* on a card and hand it to a man who is not a Christian, and they will make him mad; write these same words, *Where will you spend eternity?* on a card and hand it to a Christian, and they will make him glad. Why is it? Simply because a true believer on Jesus Christ is not afraid of, but delights in, thoughts of eternity. Why? To the one who believes on Jesus Christ, eternity is glory.

In the fourth place, the one who believes on Jesus Christ rejoices *with joy unspeakable and full of glory* because he knows he will live forever. Isn't that something to rejoice over? Isn't it wonderful? We read in 1 John 2:17: *The world passeth away, and the lust thereof: but he that doeth the will of God abideth for ever.* We all know that it is true that *the world passeth away.* We certainly ought to know it by this time; but it is equally true that *he that doeth the will of God abideth for ever.* Sometimes as we ride along our beautiful roads, we see the stately mansions of our multimillionaires, and the thought will sometimes come to us, "It must be very pleasant to live there." Well, I suppose it must be, but think for a moment. How long will these people live there? The father of the household may perhaps live there ten years, possibly twenty years. Then where does he live? Some of the children may live there twenty, thirty, possibly forty years; then what? The grave. I tell you it is not worth much after all.

But the Christian looks on and beyond to a life that has no end, to a life that is eternal. Glory!

In the fifth place, those who truly believe on Jesus Christ *rejoice greatly with joy unspeakable and full of glory* because they know they are children of God. It is a great thing to know that you are a child of God. How does the Christian know it? He knows it because God says so. *As many as received him, to them gave he the right to become children of God, even to them that believe on his name* (John 1:12 ASV). A child of God! Think of it! Sometimes as I have traveled around the world, someone has pointed out to me a man and said, "That man is the son of such and such a man (naming some king). Wouldn't you like to be the son of a great king? Just look at that young man. He is the son of a king."

In one country many years ago, when the king's business was better than it is today, I was taken up and introduced to the son of one of the reigning monarchs of Europe, and the man who introduced me whispered to me, "He is the son of So-and-so" (naming the king). Well, what of it? He was a fine man in himself, but what if he was the son of a king? I am a son of God, which is far greater, and every believer in Jesus Christ in this building is a child of God, the child of the King of Kings. And any one of you here, if you are not already a child of God, can become one in an instant by receiving the Lord Jesus.

In the sixth place, and closely connected with the last, true believers in Jesus Christ rejoice with *joy unspeakable and full of glory* because they are heirs of God, and joint-heirs with Jesus Christ. Isn't that wonderful? We are so familiar with it that we do not stop to take in the meaning of it. One of England's dukes lay dying. He called his brother to him, the one who would succeed to the title, and said, "Brother, in a few hours now you will be a duke and – and I will be a king." He was already a child

> It is a great thing to know that you are a child of God.

of the King, and in a few hours he himself would be a king. I will also be a king in a few days.

You may say, "It may be many years." Well, many years are only a few days on the scale of eternity. And, if you really are a believer in Christ Jesus, if you have a real living faith in Him, you too will be a king in a few days. There was never a royal pageant sweeping through the streets of London at any coronation comparable in glory to the glory that awaits you and me just over yonder. *When Christ, who is our life, shall be manifested, then shall ye also with him be manifested in glory* (Colossians 3:4 ASV). We may be poor today. That does not matter. This life will be over in a moment and the other life begun, and that life is eternal.

In the seventh place, those who truly believe on Jesus Christ, those who throw their hearts wide open to Him, those who surrender absolutely to Him, *rejoice greatly with joy unspeakable and full of glory* because God gives them the Holy Spirit, and there is no other joy in the present life like the joy of the Holy Spirit. One Monday morning in Chicago, my front doorbell rang. I kept Monday in those days for my rest day and had a notice above the doorbell: "Mr. Torrey does not see anyone on Monday." The maid went to the door, and there stood a poor woman. The maid said, "Mr. Torrey does not see anyone on Monday. Didn't you see the notice over the doorbell?"

She said, "I knew that, but I have got to see him, and you just go and tell him a member of his church must see him."

So the maid brought her into the reception room. She was a washerwoman. The maid showed the washerwoman a seat and came upstairs and said to me, "There is a woman downstairs who is a member of your church and says she has got to see you." So down I walked.

As I entered the room she arose and hurried toward me and said, "Mr. Torrey, I knew you did not see anybody on Monday, but I had to see you. Last night after I went to bed, I was filled with the Holy Spirit right there in my bed, and I was so happy I could not sleep all night, and this morning I had to come and tell somebody. I could not afford to give up a day's work to come around and tell you about it, but I knew I must tell somebody, and I most wanted to tell you. I know you won't be angry."

Indeed, I was not angry. I was glad she came and I rejoiced with her – that old washerwoman filled with the Holy Spirit and so full of joy that, poor as she was, she had to give up a day's work to go and tell somebody she loved all about it.

Before I came to believe on the Lord Jesus Christ, I was one of the bluest men that ever lived. I would sit down by the hour and brood. I have never known what the blues mean since the day I really became a Christian, absolutely surrendered to God. I have had troubles. I have had losses. There have been times in my life when I have lost pretty much everything the world holds dear. I know what it is to have a wife and four children and to lose everything of a financial kind I had in the world and not know from meal to meal where the next meal was coming from. I was absolutely without resources, living from hand to mouth, from God's hand to my mouth. I have known what it is to be with a wife and child in a foreign country where they spoke a strange language, and for some reason or other, supplies did not come, and I did not know anyone in the city well enough to turn to them for help, but I did not worry. I knew it was all in God's hands, that it would all come out right somehow, and of course, it did come out right.

The first time I ever visited London, thirty-nine years ago last September, I was planning to spend two weeks in England and then head to America. I expected to find money waiting for me when I reached London, and I reached London with a wife and child but not a letter and no money. But I said, "The letter and the money will come tomorrow or the next day." My wife went and made some purchases, taking it for granted we would have money when the purchases came, but the money did not come. Day after day passed, and the dresses came, and it was about time for the landlady to come with the rent bill. It came to be the very last day before our boat was to leave, and not a penny was in sight. I went down to the bank. I did not know a soul in London. There were three or four million people there at that time; I was a stranger amid three or four millions of people, money absolutely gone, three thousand miles from friends. I did not worry. I knew the money would come. I did not know how it would come, for the source I expected to receive it from seemed utterly cut off, but I was happy anyway. Why? Because I was a child of God, and I had the promises of the Bible; I knew they were absolutely sure. I never lost an hour's sleep. I never worried. I just trusted. It seemed as though I would have to be fed somewhat as Elijah was, but I knew I would be fed. I knew my wife and child would be provided for. The money came, and I sailed on the steamer that I expected to sail on with every penny that was due paid and with money in my pocket. Friends, a Christian is happy at all times and under all circumstances. We rejoice with *joy unspeakable and full of glory* every one of the twenty-four hours of the day that we are awake and sometimes in our sleep. You too can have that joy.

How to Get This Joy That Is Unspeakable and Full of Glory

Now arises the question, What must anyone do to get this *joy unspeakable and full of glory*? I have answered that question several times in what I have already said, but to be sure that we all understand it, let me answer it again, or rather let my text answer it: *On whom, though now ye see him not, yet believing, ye rejoice greatly with joy unspeakable and full of glory.* The text tells us that the way to obtain this *joy unspeakable and full of glory,* the way to be unspeakably happy at all times and under all circumstances, is just by believing on the unseen Jesus Christ.

What does it mean to believe on Jesus Christ? There is no mystery at all about that. It simply means to put confidence in Jesus Christ and believe He is what He claims to be and what He offers Himself to be for us. To believe on Jesus Christ is to put confidence in Him as the One who died in our place, the One who bore our sins in His own body on the cross, and to trust God to forgive us all our sins because Jesus Christ died in our place. To believe on Jesus Christ is to put confidence in Him as the One who was raised from the dead and who now has *all power in heaven and in earth,* and therefore is able to keep us day by day and give us victory over sin day by day. To believe on Jesus Christ is to put confidence in Him as our absolute Lord and Master, and therefore surrender our thoughts and wills and lives entirely to His con-trol, believing everything He says, even though every scholar on earth denies it. It means obeying everything He com-mands, whatever it may cost, putting our confidence in Him as our divine Lord, and confessing Him as Lord before the world as we worship and adore Him. It is wonderful the joy that comes to the one who thus believes on Jesus Christ. But one must really believe on Jesus Christ to have this joy.

> But one must really believe on Jesus Christ to have this joy.

Merely being a member of a church is not enough. Merely being baptized is not enough. Merely being confirmed is not enough. Merely reading your Bible is not enough. Merely read-ing the Prayer Book is not enough. Merely going to church is not enough. Merely partaking of the Lord's Supper is not enough. But if you are a real believer on Jesus Christ, have put all your trust in the Lord Jesus as your atoning Savior, risen

Savior, and your risen Lord and Master, you will experience *joy unspeakable.* If you have surrendered your thoughts and life to Him as your Lord and Master, and confessed Him as such before the world, and thrown your heart's door wide open for the Lord Jesus to come in, and live, and rule, and reign there, you will have *joy unspeakable and full of glory* at all times and under all circumstances.

All anyone has to do, then, to be unspeakably happy at all times and under all circumstances, is to believe on Jesus Christ. It does not make any difference what his circumstances may be: he may be rich or he may be poor; he may be highly educated or he may be ignorant; he may be in good health or he may be a hopeless invalid; he may have been a moral, clean, upright man or he may have been the vilest of sinners. It doesn't matter. Everyone who believes on the unseen but living Christ will find *joy unspeakable and full of glory.* I can bring scores, hundreds, thousands of witnesses to prove that. You cannot bring a single witness on the other side.

Colonel Robert Ingersoll delighted to say, "It does not make one happy to be a Christian." How did he know? He never tried it. You can search the earth through, and you will not find one single man or woman who was ever a believer in Jesus Christ, a real wholehearted believer in Jesus Christ, one who had surrendered all to Jesus Christ, who will deny that Jesus Christ gives *joy unspeakable and full of glory* to those who thus believe on Him. Here, then, is the way the case stands: every single competent witness, that is, every witness who has ever tried it, testifies that believing on Jesus Christ does bring *joy unspeakable and full of glory.* These witnesses number thousands, tens of thousands, and hundreds of thousands – people from every position of society and culture – and not one witness on the other side. Is it demonstrated or not? It certainly is.

I take it that I am speaking tonight to reasonable men and

women. You desire *joy unspeakable and full of glory,* and I have told you how to get it. There can be no doubt about it. The evidence is overwhelmingly convincing. There is then only one rational thing for you to do: Believe on Jesus Christ now. Will you do it?

A man came to me once who was utterly miserable. He was a rarely gifted man, a brilliant scholar, but utterly miserable. If ever I saw a man in hell, he was the man. He had attempted suicide at least four times. He had been so near to succeeding in his attempts that on two occasions it had been necessary to pump the poison he had taken out of him and thus bring him back to life. I urged him to believe on Jesus Christ. He replied, "I cannot; I have sinned away the day of grace."

Day after day I talked with the man, and I only had one message: "Come to Jesus Christ. Believe on Jesus Christ." At last, one day the man did come to Jesus Christ. He found *joy unspeakable and full of glory.* I have seen that man sometimes when his face was radiant. Out of hell into heaven by just believing on Jesus Christ. Will you take that same step tonight?

Chapter 7

Is There Any Man or Woman Whom the Lord Jesus Cannot Save and Fill with Radiant Joy?

He is able. (Hebrews 7:25)

My subject: Is there a man or woman in this city whom the Lord Jesus cannot save and fill with radiant joy? There is not. But that is merely my assertion, and I do not ask anybody to take anything on my say-so. I am going to prove conclusively to every one of you the truth of my assertion. I am going to prove so conclusively that there is not a man or woman in this city whom Jesus Christ cannot save and fill with radiant joy, that if any of you go out of this auditorium tonight unsaved or with a heavy heart, it will be your own fault. I am not going to prove it by merely quoting from the Bible. That would be enough, for the proof that the Bible is God's sure Word is overwhelming to anybody who wishes to know the truth.

But I am going prove it by what my own eyes have seen – by present-day facts that are unquestionably and demonstrably facts. But before I give you my text and my argument, I wish to tell you about three people with whom I have dealt person-ally. The first was a woman, apparently a most desperate and hopeless case. She had killed a man, and in addition to that, she was a professional murderer of infants. But that was not all. She had come one night to hear me preach and was brought under deep conviction of sin and had called at my office the next day and told me her story, and I dealt with her. But the devil was not willing to let her go so easily, and she resisted her convictions. She was not willing to yield to Jesus Christ. One afternoon she came to me at the close of my Bible class with a hard look on her face and with one of the most terrible mocking laughs I ever heard. She said, "Mr. Torrey, you cannot trouble me anymore with your preaching or your teaching. I admit that you did trouble me. I admit that my conscience was deeply stirred, but I have prayed to the devil to take away my convictions, and he has done it. Ha! Ha!" She laughed with a hard, steely look in her eyes and an evil look upon her face.

As I recall, all that I said in reply was, "Well, you are the greatest fool I have ever known." And she went away. But I prayed for her.

The second person was a man, a drunken shoemaker. He had tried to kill his wife when he was drunk, and his wife had fled with their child and was in hiding. My private secretary had put her in a place of safety. The man came to me and said, "Mr. Torrey, do you know where my wife is?"

I replied, "I do."

He said, "Tell me where she is."

I said, "I will not. You are not fit to have a wife. You tried to kill your wife last Saturday night. I will not tell you where she is."

He said, "If you do not tell me where she is, I will kill myself."

"No," I said, "you will not kill yourself. You do not dare. You are a coward. Moreover, if you do kill yourself, you will go to hell," and with that I dismissed him. But he kept coming to see me. He got under what he called "deep conviction of sin" and would come around for me to pray with him, and

I would pray with him. He would cry to God to save him from the drink. The tears would roll down his cheeks; then he would ask me for a nickel or a dime to go down to Pullman to get a job, and I knew the money all went for whiskey. He kept this up for several years. He would not only hit me up for money but he'd hit the students up also. I suppose he got hundreds of dollars out of the students. He would cry and whine and snivel, and the tears would roll down his cheeks. He would profess repentance, then hit somebody up for money and go off and get drunk; he kept up that game for years.

The third person was a man, a very gifted man, said to be the most brilliant Greek scholar and the most brilliant scholar in some other areas that one of our well-known universities had graduated for many years. But the man had gone against his conscience in many things until he was in a morbid state of mind bordering on insanity. He had attempted suicide at least five times. Morphine or other drugs had been pumped out of him two or three times. He was sent to me from Ohio to Chicago under guard lest he kill himself on the way. The man who brought him led him to me and introduced him; then he said, "May I go now?"

I said, "Yes, leave him with me."

The man sank down, glared at me, and said, "I am possessed of the devil."

I said, "I think you are. But Jesus Christ came to cast out demons."

"No," he said, "that is not what I mean. I mean the devil has entered into me as he did into Judas Iscariot."

I said, "That may be true, but Jesus Christ is stronger than the devil."

He said, "I have committed the unpardonable sin."

I said, "Jesus Christ says, *Him that cometh to me I will in no wise cast out.*"

He said, "I have no desire to come to Him."

I said, "He does not say that if anyone has a desire to come to Him, He will in no wise cast him out. He says, *Him that cometh to me I will in no wise cast out.*"

The conversation went on in that way for some time, and then I sent him to a room. For many long months, scenes like this were repeated. At times at night after the meetings, I would take him to our home three miles away on the front end of the car through a wild blizzard, hoping to cool him down. At other times in the middle of the night, I would hear somebody creeping up the stairs toward my door on the third floor, and I knew it was this man.

These three persons seemed to me at the time to be the three most hopeless cases I had ever met. So one day I said to God, "Oh God, if You will give me these three persons, if You will let me see these three persons clearly saved, I will never despair of another person as long as I live." And God allowed me to see every one of these three persons saved and filled with radiant joy.

Years have passed, more than twenty-five years, and they have all stood fast. Almost every time I pass through Chicago, if I speak anywhere in the city, this woman who had prayed to the devil and had stained her hands with human blood and had been guilty of infant murder, hears of my visit and is in my audience. She comes to me at the close with a happy, radiant face and tells me how God is using her to lead others to Christ. There are people in this audience tonight who may know her, but they do not know her history. I have never told her story to a human being in a way that they could tell who it was.

The second person, the man who tried to kill his wife and for years solicited Christian workers by prayer and weeping and got money out of them to squander in drink, is today a very active and happy member of the Moody Church with a happy wife and a son now grown to manhood. Many know his history and the details of it. The whole family often comes up to me when I go to Chicago, and all of them beam with smiles. When I held a union meeting of the churches of Chicago years afterward, he was one of my most faithful ushers.

The third person is known by many here who have heard him teach the Word of God with mighty power in Chicago, Toronto, St. Louis, Detroit, and many other cities in America and across the Pacific in China. Do you wonder, after three such experiences as these, and I could relate many more, some of which might seem more wonderful than any of these, that I never despair of anyone? Do you need to wonder why I have an unshakable confidence that there is not a man or woman in Los Angeles or anywhere else whom the Lord Jesus Christ, the omnipotent Son of God, cannot save and fill with radiant joy?

Now for my text. It consists of only three words, three short words. There are only eight letters in the whole text. You will find these three short words in Hebrews 7:25. *He is able.* The whole verse is a great verse and sums up in a wonderful way what the mighty Jesus, the risen Son of God, is able to do. It is: *Wherefore also he is able to save to the uttermost them that draw near unto God through him, seeing he ever liveth to make intercession for them* (ASV). But I wish to concentrate your attention tonight on these three words: *He is able.*

> I wish to concentrate your attention on these three words: He is able.

What Jesus Is Able to Do

Let's look at what the Lord Jesus is able to do. Let's look at some of the tremendously important specific things that He is able to do. The verse from which my text is taken sums up what He is able to do in four wonderful words: *save to the uttermost.*

Not merely *from* the uttermost (we shall see before we finish that He is able to do that), but the verse teaches far more than that. It says that *he is able to save to the uttermost.* The Greek words so translated mean "unto entire completeness," or "unto entire perfectness." But I wish to call your attention to some of the wonderful details that are included in that striking general statement, "to the uttermost" or "unto entire perfectness."

First of all, the Lord Jesus is able to forgive sins. That was His claim when He was here upon earth. He said of Himself, *The Son of man hath power on earth to forgive sins* (Mark 2:10 AKJV). He is able to forgive any sin and all sins. He Himself tells us that there is only one unpardonable sin, the blasphemy against the Holy Spirit (Matthew 12:31-32), the deliberately attributing to the devil what you know to be the work of the Holy Spirit. And it is evident from our Lord's words that the only reason that this sin is unpardonable is because the people who commit this sin are so hardened and determined in sin that they will not repent and have no desire to repent. So if anyone here has any desire to repent and be forgiven, it proves conclusively that you have not committed this one unpardonable sin. Absolutely every other sin the Lord Jesus can forgive and will forgive, if the sinner meets the one condition of forgiveness – simply putting his trust for forgiveness in the Lord Jesus.

How do we know that the Lord Jesus is able to forgive sins? Because He said He had *authority on earth to forgive sins* (Matthew 9:6 ASV) and proved on the spot that He had that authority which He claimed. Furthermore, God set the stamp of His own endorsement on this wonderful claim of Jesus Christ, and upon all of His claims, by raising Him from the dead. His resurrection from the dead is the best proven fact of history. The proof of it is overwhelming. But that is not all. Thousands upon thousands of living witnesses today bear witness to the fact that they know that the Lord Jesus has forgiven their sins.

My own sins were very many and very great, and I know that the Lord Jesus has forgiven every one of them.

Let me tell you of one instance, though not more notable than many of which I have had personal knowledge. Years ago, there was in New York City a young woman of about twenty-five years of age. She had been sold into a life of sin by her own mother at the age of eleven, and not only that, but she was also sold to a black person even though she was white. She lived this awful life in the vilest slums of New York until she was about twenty-five years old. One night a friend of mine saw her stagger up from an underground den of infamy in the Pell Street district in New York. She leaned against a lamppost and groaned in her misery. My friend stepped up to her and told her of the Lord Jesus Christ and His power to save. He sent her to a place where she would be sheltered and looked after. He led her to a definite acceptance of Jesus Christ. Her life was marvelously transformed; her every sin was blotted out. From being one of the vilest of the vile in New York, she became a remarkably beautiful Christian character.

One day she stood on the public platform in the Cooper Institute in New York, and with tears running down her cheeks, and the cheeks of her audience, pled with wonderful power to three thousand people to accept Jesus Christ. Her previous life had broken her health. She lived only about two years after her conversion, but they were wonderful years.

The night she died the man who had led her to Christ called to see her in the home where she was sheltered. As he entered the room, the smile of heaven was upon her face. A large picture of his daughter, who had died at four years of age, hung at the foot of the dying slum girl's bed. She looked at her benefactor and said, "Uncle Charlie, I shall soon see Florence." Then a brighter light came into her face, and she said, "Uncle Charlie, in a few minutes I shall see Jesus." And she departed to be with the King. Can anyone question, then, that Jesus Christ has power on earth today to forgive sins, to forgive all sins, and to wash the record of the vilest sinner on earth as white as snow?

In the second place, the Lord Jesus is able to save from sin's power. He is able to save any man from sin's power, no matter how completely he is bound or how hopelessly he is straining in his own strength to throw off the shackles of sin. How do we know that? Because the Lord Jesus Himself says so. He says, *Verily, verily, I say unto you, Every one that committeth sin is the bondservant [slave] of sin.* Now we all know that is true; we all know that it is true with all of us. We have personal experience of the fact. But our Lord also says, *If therefore the Son shall make you free, ye shall be free indeed* (John 8:36 ASV).

But our Lord Jesus not only claimed when He was on earth that He could save any man who would put his trust in Him from the power of sin and Satan, but He also proved it. No one ever came to Him for deliverance from the power of sin but that he got it. And Jesus Christ is proving today that He has power on earth today to deliver any man from the power of sin. Miracles of deliverance from sin's power are just as common today as they were when Jesus our Lord walked upon this earth.

> **Miracles of deliverance from sin's power are just as common today as they were when Jesus our Lord walked upon this earth.**

Indeed, they are more common than they were then, for then He was in His humiliation, but now He is in His resurrection glory and power (John 14:12).

I wanted to tell you of some instances that had come under my personal observation, but so many came surging into my mind that I had difficulty in deciding which to tell. There was Billy the Boozer in Cardiff, Wales, and Bob in Glasgow, Scotland, who sent a defiant letter to the platform, saying that he was in the gallery, that Jesus Christ could not save him, and that when he died and went to hell, the devil would resign and appoint him leader in his place. Then there was a man in Liverpool; there was also a woman in Dublin, who seemed the most awful woman I ever met. She must have been sixty years old, highly educated, intimately associated with people whose names were known around the world in cultured circles.

But I will tell you of a man in Minneapolis. He had once been notable in the world. He had been postmaster in his hometown. But he had gone down through drink until he was separated from his wife, children, mother, and all friends. He drifted to Minneapolis, became a beer slinger in the lowest saloon in the city, the Jumbo Saloon, but became so bad that they kicked him out of there, so he wandered on the streets. He had one small coin left in his pocket, all he had in the world, a ten-cent piece. He came down Washington Avenue drunk. He came by the brilliantly lighted hall where I was speaking and thought it was some free-lunch joint. He staggered in with his hat on the side of his head and the stub of a cigar, which he had picked out of the gutter, in his mouth. He looked confusedly around the room. A lady stepped up to him and courteously asked him if he would take off his hat and give her the stub of his cigar, which she laid aside. She brought him down to the front of the hall, right near the platform, to the only seat she could find vacant.

The speaker, another man who had been wonderfully saved from drink, was telling of the saving power of Jesus Christ. This poor down-and-out man leered up at me, lurched in his chair, and said, "Do you believe that?" referring to the testimony that the man was giving.

I said, "Yes, I know that what this man says is true, and the Lord Jesus can save you too." When the man had finished his testimony, I said, "Joe, take this man around into my office," which was at the back of the platform. After the meeting was over, he was somewhat sobered, and I led him to Christ. He left the building a saved man. The appetite that nothing else could break was broken in a moment by the power of the risen Christ. He never touched another drop of drink.

The next day he found work, peeling potatoes in a cheap restaurant. Soon he found better work. Then he was an employee of one of the leading railroads in the Northwest. He was promoted from position to position. I moved to Chicago and became the superintendent of the Bible Institute, and he was planning to come down and prepare for the ministry. But his health broke down, and the higher railway officials thought so much of him that they sent him down to Missouri to a warmer climate and paid all his expenses for months in the hope that he might recover. But he passed into glory.

After his death, his mother, to whom he had been reunited, wrote me and told me of his triumphant death. She sent me his picture, saying, "You were kind to my boy when he was down, and I want you to have this to remember him by." I wrote his story on the back of the picture and placed it on the mantelpiece in my office in Chicago. Whenever I was tempted to be discouraged, I would turn around in my chair and look at that noble Christian face looking down on me from the mantelpiece. Yes, Jesus *is able,* able to snap the bonds of drink or drugs, or lust, or any sin of any man or any woman who comes in utter helplessness to Him and puts their trust in Him to set them free.

In the third place, our Lord Jesus is able to keep us from falling. We read in Jude 24 (AKJV), He *is able to keep you from falling, and to present you faultless before the presence of his glory with exceeding joy.* Thank God that we not only read it in Jude 24, but we also read it in the experience of thousands of men and women today. Our Lord Jesus proves every day that He can keep any man or woman, any human being, from falling. I have known a multitude of men and women who have thought that there was no use for them to try to be Christians or to lead a better life because of their utter bondage to sin of some form, sometimes many forms. They thought the Lord Himself could not keep them from falling, but they were persuaded to put their trust in Him and He has kept them from falling. Let me tell you of just one.

It was in Ottawa, Canada. One afternoon there came into the meeting a most degraded-looking specimen of humanity. Someone whispered to me that he was the champion welterweight boxer of Canada and an awful drunkard. He was drunk that afternoon. Before I began to preach, I prayed that God would save him. I saw Mr. Jacoby seated beside him, and he afterwards dealt with him personally and led him to Christ. They told me that the man was such a desperate character that a saloonkeeper in Hull, across the river, had hired him to stand at the bar and drink with everyone that came in who would pay for his drinks. But knowing how dangerous he was when drunk, this saloonkeeper riveted around his ankle a heavy iron ring fastened to a heavy chain that was fastened to a great spike driven into the floor. When he professed to accept Christ, all Ottawa was amazed. But they said he would not stand.

Bets were made among the members of Parliament as to how long he would. They bet that he would not stand twenty-four hours. But he did. Then they bet that he would not stand another twenty-four hours. But he did. Then they bet that he would not stand another twenty-four hours. But he did. And they gave up betting. That man was only one out of a great multitude.

I could stand here by the hour and tell of slaves of dope, cocaine, morphine, chloral, and of other drugs. I could tell of slaves of drink, slaves of the gambling mania, slaves of impurity in every known form, and slaves of every sin of which I have ever heard. I could tell of hopeless slaves, despairing slaves, seemingly bound for a hopeless sinner's grave and an eternal hell, but these have been set free and are among the finest Christians I have ever known. I am not speculating tonight; I am not guessing; I am not theorizing. I am telling you what I know by my own personal experience and observation. I tell you that the Lord Jesus Christ is able to keep any man or woman in this building tonight from falling, if you come to Him with an honest heart and put your trust in Him as your crucified Savior from the guilt of sin, and your risen Savior from the power of sin.

In the fourth place, our Lord Jesus Christ, our mighty divine Savior, not the Savior of Unitarianism, Theosophy, Christian Science, New Thought, Higher Criticism, or New Theology, but the Savior of this Book, the risen Christ Jesus, the very Son of God, is able to completely transform the lives of men and women who put their trust in Him. This Book says *if any man be in Christ, he is a new creature [creation]: old things are passed away; behold, all things are become new* (2 Corinthians 5:17 AKJV). Yes, this Book says it, and the experience of countless multitudes proves it true. Our Lord Jesus proved in Bible days that He could completely transform men's lives by doing it.

> Our Lord Jesus proved in Bible days that He could completely transform men's lives by doing it.

For example, He transformed Saul of Tarsus, who had stained his hands with the blood of men and women and children who were guilty of no other crime than that of believing in Jesus Christ. Saul of Tarsus, who had breathed an atmosphere of *threatenings and slaughter,* was transformed into Paul the apostle, whose heart was filled with love instead of hate, and whose hands were given to saving others instead of slaughtering others. Our Lord transformed him from being Saul, a bigoted Jew, into Paul, a devoted Christian, who instead of seeking the death of others, laid down his own life to save others. This Paul toward the end of his life wrote from what he knew by his own experience as well as by inspiration of God: *This is a faithful saying, and worthy of all acceptation, that Christ Jesus came into the world to save sinners; of whom I am chief* (1 Timothy 1:15 AKJV). But the living Lord Jesus, still living in glory at the right hand of God the Father, is doing the same thing today right here on earth. Here again a crowd of memories surges before my mind. Here is just one case.

A boy of German parentage was drunk in Philadelphia when he was nine years old. At fifteen years old, no school could manage him, nor could his father and mother. He was a young desperado. He enlisted in the navy and spent four years in the navy during the Civil War. At the end of the Civil War, he was given a place on the Philadelphia police force but was so full of criminal traits himself that he was discharged from the Philadelphia police force. The mayor of the city said he would not put him on the force again if he were his own brother. He became a young outlaw in Philadelphia. He joined the regular army and was sent west in the Indian wars. He experienced some desperate encounters, not so much with Indians as with desperadoes, and he was as desperate and lawless as any of them. He spent most of his time in the guardhouse.

There was a motley company of desperadoes in the guardhouse at the time, some of the most desperate criminals in the land, and they elected him chief of the gang. He was dishonorably discharged from the army and became a notorious character. He was ordered out of the city of Omaha by the mayor and by the chief of police, and was given only twenty-four hours to leave the city, because he had nearly killed the bully of Omaha in a fight. He was invited to join the Jesse James gang. He went to an Iowa town where, because of having considerable money left to him by his father, he went into business. But he became so notoriously bad that when the merchants of the town would hear his whoop as he came up the streets at night, they would turn out the lights in their stores and put up the shutters at the windows. The town outlawed him, forced him to leave the town, and ordered him not to come back. But he came back. A revival service was then in progress. He went in with one of his cronies. When the invitation was given for all who would accept Christ to lift their hands, he said to the other man, "You lift your hand and I will lift mine."

The other man said to him, "Bill, you lift your hand and I will lift mine."

But they were both joking and ridiculing the meeting. But the next night, a man who sat in front in this church one morning a few weeks ago, a prominent lawyer, went to him and said, "Bill, come up to the altar," and he went.

And the Lord Jesus met him, saved him, and transformed him into the noblest, truest man I ever knew – the truest friend I have on earth today, the dearest friend outside of my own family. And if anyone would ask me who was the most Christlike man I ever knew, without hesitation I would say, the Reverend William S. Jacoby, who at the age of forty-two turned his back upon a notorious career of sin and accepted Jesus Christ. And our risen Lord proved His resurrection power by completely transforming that life into the likeness of His own. Oh, I know, I say I know – not guess, nor think, nor hope – I know that our Lord Jesus, our mighty, risen, divine Savior, the Savior of this man, is able to transform any life from all that is vilest into all that is noblest and highest and most divine.

In the fifth place, our mighty Lord Jesus is able to fill the saddest hearts with the most radiant joy. We read in this Book: *They looked unto him, and were radiant* (Psalm 34:5 ASV), and *though now ye see him not, yet believing, ye rejoice greatly with joy unspeakable and full of glory* (1 Peter 1:8 ASV). These words were written by one whose heart was once utterly sad and broken but was now filled *with joy unspeakable and full of glory.* Our Lord Jesus lifts men out of the deepest depths of utter despair to the highest heights of rapturous joy. Here again I remember crowds of men and women in inconsolable and utter sorrow – whom it has been my privilege to introduce to Jesus Christ – who became among the most radiantly happy people I ever knew.

I am tempted to tell you of the one I knew best and still know best of all – myself. I know what it means to be driven to such desperation by heart agony that seemed so unendurable that I started to end my own life. I have known what it means to spring out of bed with a shriek of agony and despair in the middle of the night and cower on the floor in an agony that was a very hell on earth. In

> Our Lord Jesus lifts men out of the deepest depths of utter despair to the highest heights of rapturous joy.

years gone by, I have said, "I know that there is a hell because I have been there." But thank God that for years and years this glorious Lord Jesus has filled my whole soul day and night with a continuous rapturous joy amidst all sorts of trials and perils and losses on sea and land and in nearly every corner of the earth. But I will tell of another and not myself.

There was a woman in Cleveland, Ohio, the wife of a well-to-do merchant. But financial reverses overtook the man, and he was forced to give up his business. Almost everything he had in the world was swept away. He went to Chicago to seek a new start, leaving his wife, two sons, and a daughter in Cleveland. He became sick in Chicago, and they telegraphed his wife to come. She hurried to Chicago, getting there late at night, and drove at once to the hospital where her husband lay ill, very ill. But by some strange misunderstanding, they refused to allow her to see her husband that night; being so late, they told her to come the next day. When she came early the next day, he was dead.

Money gone, business gone, husband gone, home gone. She

spent hours weeping, and her prolonged weeping injured her eyes. She called upon an eye specialist, not knowing that he was a Christian Scientist but supposing him to be a regular practitioner. Following his Christian Science methods, he assured her that there was no serious trouble with her eyes, and they would soon be all right. This was the assurance he gave her day after day. But her eyes became steadily worse, until she finally consulted a real physician. After a careful examination he said, "Madam, I am forced to tell you that there is absolutely no hope of saving your eyesight. If you had come to me sooner, your eyes could easily have been saved, but you have now waited so long that it is impossible."

In a short time she was totally blind. Money gone, business gone, home broken up, husband dead, eyesight gone! A woman of culture and refinement left to face the world with her three children and no money, no friends, no husband, no sight! Is it any wonder that her heart was filled with gloom? She came to hear me preach in Chicago. She accepted the Lord Jesus Christ. Her heartbroken soul was filled with radiant joy, and she became a radiantly happy Christian. Any prayer meeting night you could have seen her in her place, in her widow's garments and with her blind eyes, but with a wonderful smile upon her face. And oftentimes she would rise and publicly thank God for all the losses that had come into her life, because through them, she was led to the Lord Jesus Christ and to a joy she had never known when she had had all this world offered.

Years and years have passed. I received a letter from her only a short time ago, full of trust and full of longing to see others saved and helped. Our Lord Jesus can do the same tonight for the saddest heart of man or woman in this room. He can fill and flood your soul with the wondrous and perpetual sunshine of His grace. He says, *Whosoever drinketh of the water that I shall give him shall never thirst; but the water that I shall give him shall be in him a well of water springing up into everlasting life* (John 4:14 AKJV). It is true. Thousands upon thousands can testify to its truth.

People sometimes say that religion makes men and women crazy. Some forms of religion may make men and women crazy, but Jesus Christ does not make men and women crazy. He gives the Holy Spirit to those who receive Him, and *the fruit of the Spirit is love, joy, peace, longsuffering, kindness, goodness, faithfulness, meekness, self-control* (Galatians 5:22-23 ASV). Are these the things that make men and women crazy? Letting Christ into the heart has saved many men and women from insanity.

I have known many who were on the verge of insanity from sorrow, morbidness, and despair, whom I have led to Christ; they are radiantly happy people today. In order to get this fullness of joy, every Christian must make a full surrender to God. There is no fullness of joy for one who tries to serve the Lord Jesus Christ with one hand and holds fast to the world with the other hand. If we keep back anything from Jesus Christ, we will not get fullness of joy. Are you a professing Christian? Do you not have fullness of joy? There is something you are keeping back from God.

In the sixth place, our Lord Jesus Christ is able to use in glorious service those whom He saves. Our Lord Jesus is able to use the unlikeliest instrument, the man or woman of least promise. This Book tells us that *God hath chosen the foolish things of the world to confound the wise; and God hath chosen the weak things of the world to confound the things which are mighty; and base things of the world, and things which are despised, hath God chosen, yea, and things which are not, to bring to nought things that are: that no flesh should glory in his presence* (1 Corinthians 1:27-29 AKJV).

How well I remember a drunken expressman on the streets of Chicago, a Roman Catholic Irishman, a worthless wreck, but whom a personal worker led to accept Jesus Christ as his Savior. And dear Cully became one of the most useful soul winners in Chicago. It was one of the greatest privileges of my life to be able to do honor to my Lord, and honor to myself, by conducting his funeral service to which multitudes flocked.

In the last place, our Lord Jesus, the risen, mighty Son of God, is able to raise from the dead, and to give eternal life to all who put their trust in Him in the life that now is. He Himself says, *And this is the will of him that sent me, that of all that which he hath given me I should lose nothing, but should raise it up at the last day. For this is the will of my Father, that every one that beholdeth the Son, and believeth on him, should have eternal life; and I will raise him up at the last day* (John 6:39-40 ASV).

He also says in that wonderful prayer of His on the night before His crucifixion, *These things spake Jesus; and lifting up his eyes to heaven, he said, Father, the hour is come; glorify thy Son, that the Son may glorify thee: even as thou gavest him authority over all flesh, that to all whom thou hast given him, he should give eternal life* (John 17:1-2 ASV).

It is true that the wonderful and glorious work of *the great God and our Saviour Jesus Christ* (Titus 2:13) does not end at death. It begins there; the best part of it begins there. Oh, the salvation that is limited to this life is not worth much. This life is so short. And eternity is so long. A brief lifetime of bitter disappointment, sorrow, loss, and intense and constant suffering would pay off if it would bring us an eternity of joy, victory, and glory. But Jesus Christ brings a whole lifetime of joy, peace, and power, and an eternity also of boundless joy, abounding peace, amazing power, and

> Jesus Christ brings a whole lifetime of joy, peace, and power, and an eternity also of boundless joy, abounding peace, amazing power, and glory hereafter.

glory hereafter. He is indeed *able to save to the uttermost them that draw near unto God through him.*

For Whom Does Our Lord Jesus Do These Things?

Now let's ask the all-important question: For whom does our glorious Lord Jesus do these things of which we have been speaking? Whom does He *save to the uttermost* and fill with radiant joy in the life that now is, and crown with infinite glory in the never-ending life that is to come? The question can be answered in a few words. Our text answers it, and the uniform experience of thousands upon thousands of men and women answers it the same way. Listen to the text: *He is able to save to the uttermost them that draw near unto God through him* (Hebrews 7:25 ASV). He saves to the uttermost *them that draw near unto God through him* – all of them and no one else. He will save anyone here and fill them with radiant joy tonight – anyone here – any man, woman, or child who will *draw near unto God through him.* It matters not who you are. It matters not what you have done. It matters not how helpless and hopeless a slave of any sin you may be. It matters not how dark, sad, and full of foreboding and despair your heart may be. Draw near unto God through Jesus Christ, and He will save you right now, and He will fill your heart with radiant joy right now.

What does it mean to *draw near unto God through him*? The answer is simple. God is a holy God, and you and I are sinners. And the only way a sinner can approach a holy God is on the ground of atoning blood, and Jesus Christ has shed His blood to atone for our sins. His blood is the only atonement for sins in the whole universe. He has *redeemed us from the curse of the law, having become a curse for us* (Galatians 3:13 ASV). In other words, He did it by taking our place and bearing our penalty. For the sinner, to come to God through Jesus Christ is acknowledging himself as a lost sinner with no hope in himself or in man, but believing what God says about Jesus Christ. It means that He has laid all our sins upon Christ, and the sinner must trust God to forgive all his sins, because Jesus Christ died in his place. There is no other way for the sinner to approach God. If anyone will not come to God through Jesus Christ, he cannot come to God at all. The vilest sinner this world ever knew who will believe God's testimony about Jesus Christ and God's testimony about Himself, who will take his place as a lost sinner before God, and trust God for Jesus Christ's sake to forgive his sins will find salvation. For He *is able to save to the uttermost them that draw near unto God through him, seeing he ever liveth to make intercession for them.*

> If anyone will not come to God through Jesus Christ, he cannot come to God at all.

These things that I have been mentioning are some of the things that our Lord Jesus is able to do for you tonight. Will you let Him do them for you? Will you come to God *through Him* that He may do them for you? Will you accept God's testimony about yourself, that you are an utterly lost sinner, and God's testimony about Jesus Christ, that He has borne your sins in His own body on the cross? Will you accept Jesus Christ as your Savior, your Lord, and your King? If you will, Jesus Christ, the mighty Son of God, will do these things for you that we have been mentioning.

It rests with each of you individually to say whether you will have your sins forgiven tonight. The Lord Jesus stands by your side and says, "I am able to forgive all your sins tonight. Trust me and I will do it." It rests with each of you individually to say whether you will have deliverance from sin's power. The Lord Jesus, the mighty Deliverer, stands by your side and says, "I am able to deliver you from the power of every sin." Ask Him to do it and trust Him to do it. Put your trust in Him as your risen

Lord and Savior, who has all power in heaven and on earth. Trust Him to set you free from every sin, and He will do it.

It rests with each of you individually to say whether you will know the transforming power of Jesus Christ in your life tonight, transforming you from all that you should not be but which you are, into all that you should be and all that you can become by faith in Jesus Christ. Jesus Christ stands right by you tonight and says, "I am able to completely transform your life, if you will put it in my hands and trust me to do it." It rests with each of you individually to say whether you will have your heart filled with radiant joy or not. Oh, this mighty Giver of the Holy Spirit, who becomes to each one who receives Him a fountain of water springing up every day and every hour unto everlasting life. He leans down beside you and holds out to you the golden goblet that contains the water of life. And if you will put your trust in Him as your crucified and risen Savior who bore all your sins in His own body on the cross, and ask Him, and trust Him to give you His Holy Spirit to fill you with radiant joy, He will do it.

It rests with each of you individually to say whether you will receive the sure guarantee of being raised again when you die, and of receiving eternal life, joy that never ends, and the hope of infinite power and glory. That mighty One, whom God has appointed to give eternal life to those who put their trust in Him and raise them up at the last day, stands by your side and says, "I will give eternal life and resurrection. Will you accept it as a free gift?" And if you will believe His word and put your trust in Him, He will give you eternal life, and you will never perish, and all the powers of earth and hell cannot pluck you out of His hand (John 10:28-29). *He is able! He is able! He is able!*

Will you come to Him? Will you put your trust in Him?

Will you surrender fully to Him? Will you put yourself in His hands to do with you as He will? Will you draw near unto God through Jesus Christ? If you do, you will get all these things. He will save you to the uttermost and fill your heart with radiant joy. If you do not, there will be barrenness and bitterness, sorrow and emptiness, despair and spiritual death, gloom and agony, and gnashing of teeth in impotent rage and sorrow throughout all eternity for you.

Chapter 8

The Unpardonable Sin

Wherefore I say unto you, All manner of sin and blasphemy shall be forgiven unto men: but the blasphemy against the Holy Ghost shall not be forgiven unto men. And whosoever speaketh a word against the Son of man, it shall be forgiven him: but whosoever speaketh against the Holy Ghost, it shall not be forgiven him, neither in this world, neither in the world to come. (Matthew 12:31-32 AKJV)

This passage is often regarded as one of the darkest and gloomiest in the Bible. Many have gone insane, or nearly insane, over this passage; or rather, being already diseased in mind, their diseased brains have seized upon this passage to brood over. But if we look at the passage carefully, we will see that the passage has its bright side, and on its bright side it is one of the most cheerful utterances that ever fell from the lips of Jesus Christ. It tells us plainly and positively that of all the sins that men or women can commit, only one sin puts a man or woman beyond hope. There is only one sin that God will not and cannot forgive if men repent and turn to Jesus Christ;

that sin is, as far as my experience goes, one that very few men and very few women have committed.

I have had countless people come to me personally and write to me from all parts of the earth, who thought they had committed this sin. Of all these who have come to me or written to me, when I questioned them carefully, it was evident that not one person among them had committed this sin. And most of those who have come to me thinking they have committed this sin have come into a bright Christian experience; many of them have since become some of the brightest and most useful Christians I have ever known.

Of all the men I have ever led to Jesus Christ, the one who has had the largest usefulness of all, usefulness not only in America but also in England, China, and elsewhere, was one who was sure that he had committed the unpardonable sin. He had attempted suicide five times, which required poison to be pumped out of him several times. His life was barely saved, and he was sent to me – hundreds of miles away under guard, for fear he would commit suicide on the way.

There Is Only One Unpardonable Sin

The first thing that our Lord Jesus makes very plain in the words that we have taken for our text is that there is only one unpardonable sin. He says, *All manner of sin and blasphemy shall be forgiven unto men: but the blasphemy against the Holy Ghost shall not be forgiven unto men*. Language could not make it plainer that in the whole catalog of possible sins, there is only one that men can commit that makes pardon and salvation impossible. Even murder, as desperate and awful a sin as it is, is not unpardonable. There have been many men and women who have stained their hands with human blood but have afterwards found pardon and eternal life and have joined the truest and noblest of Christians. I have met quite a number of persons who thought that salvation was impossible for them because they had taken the life of another man, but our Lord Jesus declares that there is only one unpardonable sin, and that unpardonable sin is not murder.

David committed murder, one of the most dastardly murders in history, and yet David found pardon. It was after he had caused the death of Uriah, his faithful soldier, that he wrote the following words: *Blessed is he whose transgression is forgiven, whose sin is covered. Blessed is the man unto whom Jehovah imputeth not iniquity, and in whose spirit there is no guile. When I kept silence, my bones wasted away through my groaning all the day long. For day and night thy hand was heavy upon me: my moisture was changed as with the drought of summer. I acknowledged my sin unto thee, and mine iniquity did I not hide: I said, I will confess my transgressions unto Jehovah; and thou forgavest the iniquity of my sin* (Psalm 32:1-5 ASV).

Saul of Tarsus, who later became Paul the apostle, was a murderer. He was responsible for the death of men, women, and children whose only fault was that they believed on the Lord Jesus Christ, and yet he found pardon. The grossest moral impurity is not unpardonable. Moral impurity is loathsome, but it is not unpardonable. Our Lord declares that there is only one unpardonable sin, and the sin He describes is not moral impurity.

I once spoke to a man at the close of my Bible class in Chicago. I stepped up to him and asked him if he was a Christian, and he said no, he was not, though he would like to be. I asked him why he was not a Christian, and with tears running down his face, he said that he had committed a sin for which there was no pardon. I told him there was only one sin for which there was no pardon, and I asked him what the sin was that he had committed for which he thought there was no pardon. He told me what it was, describing it fully. It was gross immorality. When he finished, I said, "The Bible nowhere says there is no pardon for that sin."

"But" he replied, "I remember my mother read a passage in the Bible when I was a boy that said if a man committed that sin he could not be pardoned."

"No," I said, "there is no such passage."

But he was sure that there was. I racked my brain to think what passage he might have had in mind, and suddenly it flashed upon me. I said, "Oh, I think I know the passage to which you refer." I opened my Bible and read, *Know ye not that the unrighteous shall not inherit the kingdom of God? Be not deceived: neither fornicators, nor idolaters, nor adulterers, nor effeminate, nor abusers of themselves with men, nor thieves, nor covetous, nor drunkards, nor revilers, nor extortioners, shall inherit the kingdom of God* (1 Corinthians 6:9-10 ASV).

His sin was in that dreadful list, and he said, "That is the passage. Doesn't it say that the one who commits this sin shall not inherit the kingdom of God?"

I said, "Let me read you the next verse," and I read, *And such were some of you: but ye were washed, but ye were sanctified, but ye were justified in the name of the Lord Jesus Christ, and in the Spirit of our God* (1 Corinthians 6:11 ASV).

"Does it say that?" he cried.

I said, "Look at it," and I put the Book in his hand.

He read, "*And such were some of you: but ye were washed, but ye were sanctified, but ye were justified.* Thank God, thank God," he exclaimed. Right there he accepted Christ. A few weeks later he brought his wife to Chicago, whom he had deserted in Indianapolis to go off into his life of sin. He introduced her and his grown daughter to me, and they accepted Christ. He is today an officer in the Chicago Avenue church and one of the most earnest men in the church.

Profanity and blasphemy are not unpardonable, except the one blasphemy against the Holy Spirit. The most outrageous and blatant infidelity are not unpardonable.

Before his conversion, Saul of Tarsus was a blasphemer and a foul infidel as far as Jesus Christ was concerned. Far from believing Him to be the Son of God, he believed Him to be an impostor. He says of himself that before his conversion he was a blasphemer, and a persecutor, and injurious, but the Lord Jesus had saved him (1 Timothy 1:13). In view of this, he exclaims, *This is a faithful saying, and worthy of all acceptation, that Christ Jesus came into the world to save sinners, of whom I am chief* (1 Timothy 1:15 AKJV).

> **Profanity and blasphemy are not unpardonable, except the one blasphemy against the Holy Spirit.**

What Is the Unpardonable Sin?

We come then to the question, What is the unpardonable sin?

First of all, the unpardonable sin is a definite act. It is not a certain attitude of mind; it is an act. It is not a series of actions, though it may be the outcome of a series of actions; it is one definite act. This is evident from our Lord's words: *If any man see his brother sinning a sin not unto death, he shall ask, and God will give him life for them that sin not unto death. There is a sin unto death* (1 John 5:16 ASV). The unpardonable sin, the sin unto death, is one definite sin.

Furthermore, the unpardonable sin is a sin of which one may know definitely whether he has committed it or not. A great many fear that they have committed the unpardonable sin. They are not sure that they have. They are not at all clear as to what the one unpardonable sin may be. But the unpardonable sin is a sin of such a definite and clearly defined character that one may know with certainty whether he has committed it or not.

What is this definite act? What is this one unpardonable sin? This definite unpardonable sin our Lord Jesus Christ tells us in so many words is the blasphemy against the Holy Spirit. He says, *Wherefore I say unto you, All manner of sin and blasphemy shall be forgiven unto men: but the blasphemy against the Holy Ghost shall not be forgiven unto men. And whosoever speaketh a word against the Son of man, it shall be forgiven him: but whosoever speaketh against the Holy Ghost, it shall not be forgiven him, neither in this world, neither in the world to come* (Matthew 12:31-32 AKJV).

So it is evident that the one definite unpardonable sin is the definite blasphemy against the Holy Spirit. What is blasphemy against the Holy Spirit? The context in which these words are found will tell us. The Pharisees had seen the miracles of the Lord Jesus Christ; they had seen His works of divine power and heard His words of divine grace. They had seen in these miracles clear evidence that Jesus was a teacher sent from God who spoke the very words of God (John 3:2) – that He was the Messiah, the Christ. They had been unwilling to accept Him as such, because of what it would cost them to accept Him. They had refused to accept or acknowledge Him as the Christ. But the evidence that He was the Christ was so overwhelming that at last, in their determination not to accept Him, they had deliberately attributed His works, which was of the Holy Spirit, to the devil. They had said, as recorded in this chapter in the immediate context, *This fellow doth not cast out devils, but by Beelzebub the prince of the devils* (Matthew 12:24 AKJV). In other words, they had deliberately attributed to the devil what was of the Holy Spirit. This, then, is the unpardonable sin, the only unpardonable sin, the deliberately ascribing to the devil what you distinctly know to be the work of the Holy Spirit.

It is not merely the attributing to the devil what is the work of the Holy Spirit, but also what you distinctly know to be the work of the Holy Spirit. Have you committed this sin? Have you deliberately attributed to the devil work that you distinctly know to be the work of the Holy Spirit? You reply, "I have been a great sinner." That is not my question. Have you definitely attributed to the devil what you distinctly know to be the work of the Holy Spirit? If not, then you have not committed the unpardonable sin, and there is pardon and salvation for you tonight if you will turn from your sin, whatever it may be, and accept the Lord Jesus Christ.

"But," you say, "I have sinned against the light; I have resisted the Holy Spirit." That is not the point. You may have done all this, but have you definitely attributed to the devil what you distinctly knew to be the work of the Holy Spirit? Many have sinned against the light; many have resisted the Holy Spirit. I did for years, but thank God I had not blasphemed the Holy Spirit. I had not attributed to the devil what I distinctly knew to be the work of the Holy Spirit, and I found pardon and am a saved man tonight.

"But," you will say, "I have sinned so long that I fear I have sinned away the day of grace. My heart is hard and nothing moves it now. I have no desire to repent." That is not the question. One may do all these things, and many have done all these things but have turned to Christ and found pardon. The question is, Have you deliberately and intentionally attributed to the devil what you distinctly knew to be the work of the Holy Spirit?

Whatever else you may have done, you have not committed the unpardonable sin. You may even have cursed the name of Jesus, but there is forgiveness even for that (Mark 3:28). There is pardon for you tonight – pardon for you and salvation for you before you leave this building if you turn your back upon sin and accept the Lord Jesus Christ. There is but one unpardonable sin, and you have not committed that. As I say, if you turn from your other sins, whatever they may be, and turn to God and to Christ, even without one bit of feeling, you will be saved tonight. The apostle Peter said, *To him [Jesus] bear all the prophets witness, that through his name every one that believeth on him shall receive remission of sins* (Acts 10:43 ASV). And John said that *as many as received him, to them gave he the right to become children of God, even to them that believe on his name* (John 1:12 ASV).

Why Is the Blasphemy against the Holy Spirit Unpardonable?

There is another important question for us to consider: Why is the blasphemy against the Holy Spirit unpardonable?

First, the blasphemy against the Holy Spirit is unpardonable because it indicates such a determined choice of evil that a man's character is determined finally and forever in evil. A man will not deliberately attribute to the devil what he distinctly knows to be the work of the Spirit of God unless he has settled it finally and forever that he will not accept the truth; so the man dooms himself to eternal sinfulness and eternal punishment. Such a sin comes at the end of a course of persistent rejection of the truth and persistent rejection of Jesus Christ.

> If any man will repent and come to Christ, he will be saved; the Lord Jesus Christ has declared in the most unmistakable terms.

This sin is also unpardonable because the one who deliberately commits such a sin so determines his character that repentance becomes impossible. If any man will repent and come to Christ, he will be saved; the Lord Jesus Christ has declared in the most unmistakable terms, *Him that cometh to me I will in no wise cast out* (John 6:37). But the man who commits this unpardonable sin has determined that he will not come to Christ and therefore does not come to Christ, so he cannot be pardoned.

The fact that one is concerned about his spiritual condition, the fact that one is troubled about his sins, and the fact that one desires to come to Christ are of themselves conclusive proof that one has not as yet committed the unpardonable sin. On the other hand, all conscious continuance in sin, all deliberate refusal to listen to the truth, all deliberate refusal to accept the Lord Jesus Christ when you know that you ought to accept Him, and all turning a deaf ear to the voice of the Holy Spirit are steps toward the unpardonable sin. This was the course of conduct that led the Pharisees of our text to commit the unpardonable sin. Before their very eyes, they had conclusive proof that Jesus was what He claimed to be; time and again they were moved to accept Him, but they would not. Time and again, they said no to the voice of the Spirit of God, and they had so hardened themselves in the rejection of Christ that at last in deliberate determination, they had attributed His words to the devil and became utterly blinded in mind and utterly incapable of repentance.

And some of you are pursuing exactly the same course tonight. Time and again you have been moved by the Holy Spirit to accept Christ; time and again you have said no to the voice of the Spirit of God, as He urges you to realize the necessity of forsaking your sins and accepting Christ. You are walking straight toward the unpardonable sin and toward a hopeless and eternal hell. Everyone here tonight who has heard the gospel before and refused it, and everyone who knows that Jesus Christ is the Son of God but refuses to accept Him as their Savior, is confirming themselves in sin. Everyone who has been moved by the Holy Spirit once, twice, three times, and perhaps more frequently in the past and has said no every time, every time you say no to the Holy Spirit, you are coming more surely to the point where you will commit the unpardonable sin, and your destiny will be eternally sealed.

Some years ago, there was a great religious awakening in one of our colleges. Many turned to Christ. Two young men were under deep conviction, but they would not yield. In their determination not to yield, they agreed together that on a certain night they would meet at the college chapel and go into the chapel together and blaspheme the Holy Spirit. At the appointed hour, they met in front of the chapel. The heart of one of them failed him, and he repented and turned to the Lord Jesus Christ; he was saved. The other one went into the chapel alone. No one ever knew what he did in there, but when he came out, he was as pale as a ghost. He went into utter infidelity, became one of the leaders of the infidel society in Chicago, lived many years, and died as he had lived; he was everlastingly lost.

The Spirit of God is speaking to many of you too. He has spoken to you often before. You know you ought to accept Christ. You know you ought to confess Him. If tonight you say no to Him again, you may so conclude yourself in sin that repentance will become impossible and you will be lost forever. You will be as surely lost for all eternity as when you have been in hell ten million years. On the other hand, anyone here tonight who will accept Christ, no matter what your past may have been, no matter how grossly you may have sinned, no matter how frightful your sins may have been, no matter how long you have sinned, if you will come to Christ now, there is pardon, salvation, and eternal life for you. Will you yield and accept Jesus Christ right now?

Chapter 9

The Blood of Jesus Christ, God's Son, Cleanses from All Sin

If we walk in the light, as he is in the light, we have
fellowship one with another, and the blood of Jesus
his Son cleanseth us from all sin. (1 John 1:7 ASV)

One week ago, we saw that Jesus is the Christ, the Son of God. Tonight we shall see that the blood of Jesus, whom we saw to be the Son of God, cleanses certain persons from every trace of sin, and we shall see also how we ourselves can become such persons as are cleansed from every trace of sin by the blood of Christ Jesus.

How We Know That the Blood Of Jesus Cleanses from All Sin

The first question that confronts us tonight is, How do we know that the blood of Jesus cleanses from every trace of sin?

First, we know that the blood of Jesus cleanses from every trace of sin because the Bible says so, and we have seen on former occasions that the whole Bible is the Word of God, and everything it says is undoubtedly and unqualifiedly true. I have no hesitation in believing without any qualification, reduction, discount, or attempt at a spiritualizing and vaporizing evasion of its plain meaning everything this Book says, or to be more exact and definite, everything that God, *who cannot lie,* says in this Book. In our text we read what God says, not what John says, but what God says: *The blood of Jesus his Son cleanseth us from all sin.*

Practically the same thought is found in Ephesians 1:7 (ASV): *We have our redemption through his blood, the forgiveness of our trespasses, according to the riches of his grace.* God tells us here through Paul that the believer in Jesus Christ has *redemption,* in other words, the forgiveness of his sins through the blood of Jesus Christ. Forgiveness of sin is not something the believer in Christ is to get at some time in the future when he has gone through purgatory or when he has struggled long and successfully against his sinful tendencies and against his temptations. He does not get it when he comes to die or when the Lord Jesus comes back again. Forgiveness of sins is something the believer in Jesus Christ gets because of the atoning sacrifice of the blood of Christ. He receives that forgiveness the moment he accepts Jesus Christ as his own personal Savior, the One who made perfect atonement for his sins on the cross of Calvary. When he surrenders to Jesus as his Lord and Master and confesses Him as such before the world, forgiveness is his.

Forgiveness of sins is something the believer in Jesus Christ gets because of the atoning sacrifice of the blood of Christ.

Forgiveness of sin is something anyone in this audience tonight can get right now. Anyone can know that every sin he ever committed, or ever shall commit, every sin great or small, the blackest sin that any man or woman could ever commit, and the smallest sin he ever did commit, are all blotted out of God's book and out of God's remembrance forever. Oh, this precious gospel is needed by every one of us, needed by you fine women who smugly admire your own immaculate virtue, as well as by the woman upon whom you would scarcely condescend to wipe your feet because of her disgusting vileness and indescribable shame. This gospel is needed by you Nathanaels, *Israelite[s] indeed, in whom is no guile* (John 1:47), as well as by the publican who strikes his breast and cries, *God be merciful to me a sinner* – the consummate sinner (Luke 18:13 AKJV).

The same thought is found in Romans 5:9: *Being now justified by his blood.* God tells us here through Paul that every believer in Christ is *now justified* – not justified at some future time when he gets wholly sanctified or gets through purgatory, or when he dies and gets to heaven. He is justified the moment he believes. *Justified* means more than forgiven, it means "reckoned righteous." The whole verse means that God not only forgives, dismisses from His memory every sin the believer in Christ has ever committed, but that He also puts the perfect propitiation for sin to the believer's account because of the shed blood of Christ (Romans 3:25-26). All His absolutely perfect righteousness as exhibited in the life of Jesus Christ, God manifested in the flesh, God delivered to the believer's account. Or as Paul puts it in 2 Corinthians 5:21 (ASV): *Him who knew no sin he [God] made to be sin on our behalf; that we might become the righteousness of God in him.*

When Jesus the Son of God shed His blood on the cross and thus made a perfect *propitiation for our sins* (1 John 2:2), a propitiation perfectly acceptable to God, He took our proper place of curse and condemnation and rejection before God. The moment we take Him, we step into His place of perfect acceptance before God, and God looks at us – no matter how vile we may have been – through Jesus, and sees us covered all over from head to foot with His own perfect and glorious righteousness.

If the vilest woman in Los Angeles would come in here, accept Jesus Christ as her personal Savior, surrender to Him as her Lord and Master, and confess Him as such before the world, the moment she did, every sin she had ever committed would be blotted out. She would be as perfect in her standing before God as the purest woman in this room. Some years ago I was preaching one Sunday morning in the Moody Church in Chicago on Romans 8:1 (ASV): *There is therefore now no condemnation to them that are in Christ Jesus.* I made this remark: "If the vilest woman in Chicago should come into the Chicago Avenue church this morning and should right now accept Jesus Christ as her Savior, the moment she did, every sin she ever committed would be blotted out. Her record would be as white in God's sight as that of the purest woman in the room."

Unbeknownst to me, one of the women of my congregation had gone out that very morning to one of the lowest dens of infamy in the city and sought out a woman, an utter outcast, and invited her to come to the church to hear me preach. But the woman replied, "Church is not for the likes of me. I would not be welcomed at church."

To this the pure woman replied, "You would be welcomed at our church," which, thank God, was true.

But the woman said, "No, church is not for the likes of me."

Then the pure woman said, "If you will go with me, I will go with you."

"No," the woman who was a sinner said, "that would never do. The police know me, and the boys on the streets know me and sometimes throw stones at me. If they should see you going up the street with me, they would think you were just such as I am."

But the woman who was a saint said, "I don't care what they think about me; if you will go with me, I will go with you."

But the woman would not consent. At last, they agreed on

this: that the woman who was a saint would walk a few steps ahead, and the woman who was a sinner would come a few steps behind. So on they came, block after block, up LaSalle Avenue – the woman who was a saint a few steps ahead, and the woman who was a sinner a few steps behind. At last they reached the Moody Church. The woman who was a saint ascended the stairs, entered the auditorium, and took a seat. The woman who was a sinner followed, timidly pushed open the door, saw one vacant seat in the last row under the gallery, and slipped into it. She had scarcely taken her seat when I made the statement, which I have just quoted: "If the vilest woman in Chicago should come into the Chicago Avenue church this morning and should right now accept Jesus Christ as her Savior, the moment she did, every sin she ever committed would be blotted out. Her record would be as white in God's sight as that of the purest woman in this room." My words went floating down over the heads of the audience and dropped down into the heart of this woman who was a sinner in the last seat underneath the gallery. She saw Jesus hanging on the cross in her place; she put her trust in Him, and God forgave her right there and put to her account all the righteousness of Jesus Christ. When the meeting was over, she came down the aisle, weeping, to meet me and to thank me for what God had done for her that morning.

In the second place, we know by the experience of thousands that the blood of Jesus Christ cleanses from all sin. Thousands upon thousands of sinners, some of them among the wickedest men and women that ever walked this earth, have testified of their cleansing like Paul who rightfully said that he was the *chief* of sinners. Paul had stained his hands with the blood of a multitude of men, women, and children whose only crime was that they obeyed and confessed their rightful Lord Jesus Christ (1 Timothy 1:15-17). I say there are thousands upon thousands of sinners, including many of the worst this sinful world has ever known, who testify that the blood of Jesus Christ has cleansed them from all sin, and that the Holy Spirit today is bearing witness together with their spirit that they are children of God (Romans 8:16).

If there is anything absolutely sure in this old world that is so full of doubt and uncertainty, it is that the blood of Jesus cleanses from all sin. Let subtle and self-satisfied infidels and theologians speculate and split hairs to their hearts' content as to what is philosophical and what is not, what is possible and what is not, what is God's Word and what is not God's Word. But this fact, not theological or philosophical speculation but fact, stands absolutely and eternally sure: *the blood of Jesus his Son cleanseth us from all sin.* That is not something I guess, but something I know. I know it because God says so, and He *cannot lie,* and I know it by blessed personal experience. Years ago, I pumped my head full of a lot of evolutionary and other unproven and senseless philosophy, but even that was not able to drown out what I knew: the blood of Jesus had cleansed me from all sin. Praise God!

What Does the Bible Mean When It Says the Blood of Jesus Cleanses Us from All Sin?

Now we come to the second question: What does the Bible mean when it says that *the blood of Jesus his Son cleanseth us from all sin*? The Bible makes it as clear as day. One of the many wonderful things about this wonderful Book of God is that it interprets its own statements in an unmistakable way and therefore does not leave us at the mercy of priests or popes or any unconverted, unregenerated, sin-blinded theologians, Protestant or Roman Catholic, to get our interpretations. Those theologians are the ones that the subtle old Enemy, the devil, has succeeded in packing some of our theological seminaries with.

What then does the Bible mean when it says that *the blood of Jesus his Son cleanseth us from all sin*? To be more specific, does it mean that the blood of Jesus cleanses believers from the guilt their sins bring upon them, or does it mean that the blood of Jesus cleanses the believer from the very presence of sin itself? I say that the Bible itself answers these questions in unmistakable terms. If you will take your Bible and your concordance and look up every passage in the Bible where the word *cleanse* is used in connection with the word *blood,* you will find that in every instance, cleansing by blood is cleansing from guilt. We of course don't have time to read every single passage tonight, for they are very many, but if you will come to me at the close of this meeting, I will tell you where to find them. You can look them up for yourself and be convinced (Leviticus 14:19-31; 16:30; 17:11; Jeremiah 33:8; Psalm 51:7; Revelation 1:5; 7:14; Hebrews 9:22-23; Ephesians 1:7; Romans 3:25; 5:9; Matthew 26:28).

The thought, then, of our text, interpreted in the light of the uniform and unvarying teaching of the Bible, Old Testament and New Testament, is that all who *walk in the light* are cleansed continuously. The present tense of *cleanse* is used, denoting continuous action; they are cleansed every day and every hour and every minute from all the guilt of sin. There is not one spot or trace of sin upon them in God's reckoning. There is absolutely no sin upon them, not one smallest speck. In moments of weakness and failure, there may still be sin in their conduct, but there is not one smallest sin on them in God's reckoning. It has all been settled, atoned for, and washed away forever by the atoning blood of Christ, shed on Calvary's accursed tree. It is not the blood of the crucified Jesus, but the indwelling life of the risen Jesus that saves from the power of sin. It will be the complete transforming power of the returning Lord Jesus, who will make us like Himself when He comes again (1 John 3:1-2); this power will save us from the very presence of sin. But tonight, right now, any man, woman, or child, no matter how long you may have continued in sin or how deeply you may have gone into sin, can be cleansed from every trace of guilt and become as absolutely sinless in God's reckoning as Jesus Christ Himself is. You can become:

> Near, so very near to God,
>> Nearer I cannot be;
> For in the person of His Son,
>> I'm just as near as He.
> Dear, so very dear to God,
>> Dearer I cannot be;
> For in the person of His Son,
>> I am just as dear as He.[2]

Who Is It That the Blood of Jesus Cleanses from All Sin?

Now there is just one more question, and it is one of great practical importance for us to answer, or rather for us to get God's answer to: Who is it that the blood of Jesus cleanses from all sin? The text answers this question also. Listen: *If we walk in the light, as he is in the light, we have fellowship one with another, and the blood of Jesus his Son cleanseth* **us** *from all sin* (emphasis added).

First, please notice the word *us* in *cleanseth us from all sin.* Who are meant by the *us?* God Himself answers the question in the same book: *These things have I written unto you,*

---

2   "A Mind at Perfect Peace with God," adapted from the lyrics (public domain) of Horatius Bonar by Catesby Paget (19th century).

. . . even unto you that believe on the name of the Son of God
(1 John 5:13 ASV). The *us,* then, are those who *believe on the*
name of the Son of God. But what does it mean to *believe on*
the name of the Son of God? Again, we are not left to our own
speculations and guesses, but God Himself answers this question in John 1:12 (ASV): *As many as received him, to them gave*
he the right to become children of God, even to them that believe
on his name.

It is, then, those who receive Jesus that are the ones who
believe on the name of the Son of God. They take Him to be what
He offers Himself to be to everyone and
anyone. They take Him to themselves
to be their personal Savior by carrying
their sins in His own body on the cross;
they trust God to forgive them because
Jesus died in their place, and they take
Him as their Lord and King to whom
they surrender the entire control of

> Anyone who thus
> takes or receives Jesus
> believes on Him as the
> Son of God, and the
> blood of Jesus cleanses
> them from all sin.

their thoughts and lives. Anyone who thus takes or receives
Jesus believes on Him as the Son of God, and the blood of Jesus
cleanses them from all sin.

In the second place, notice what is said in the verse which
we have taken for our text: *If we walk in the light, as he is in*
the light, we have fellowship one with another, and the blood of
Jesus his Son cleanseth us from all sin. What does it mean to
walk in the light? The truth is light; error is darkness. The truth
revealed in this Book is light; God is light (1 John 1:5); Jesus
Himself is the Light of the World (John 8:12). To walk in the
light is therefore to walk in obedience to the truth, to walk as
He whom we have accepted as our Lord and Master and risen
Savior bids us to walk and empowers us to walk. To walk in
the light is to walk in open confession of Christ, in obedience
to His will as He reveals it in His Word, and to walk just as

everyone who believes on His name (not merely professes to believe on His name) will walk.

If anyone here, no matter what you have been in the past, even though you have been the vilest moral leper, thug, gunman, most outrageous infidel or blasphemer, if any man, woman, or child will right here and now accept Jesus Christ as your personal Savior, you will be cleansed. If you trust God to forgive you because Jesus died in your place, and if you will surrender to Him as your Lord and King and confess Him as such tonight, you can go out of here and prove the reality of your faith by walking in the light. You certainly will walk in the light if you really accept Him as your crucified and risen Savior. The instant you do this, *the blood of Jesus* will cleanse you from all sin and keep cleansing you to all eternity. But if you do not do this, you will go out of here tonight utterly defiled by the guilt of your awful sins, far more awful in the sight of a holy God than you think, defiled and dishonored and accursed by the guilt of these sins forever and ever.

Will you accept Him now?

Chapter 10

Paths to Perdition

Enter ye in at the strait gate: for wide is the gate, and broad is the way, that leadeth to destruction, and many there be which go in thereat: because strait is the gate, and narrow is the way, which leadeth unto life, and few there be that find it.
(Matthew 7:13-14 AKJV)

Two classes of people are in this audience: those who are on the narrow road that leads to life, and those who are on some other path that makes up the one broad road that leads to perdition, *eternal perdition*. Some people say, "Let's go with the crowd." Well, if you go with the crowd, you will go to hell. Listen again to the words of Jesus Christ: *Enter ye in at the strait gate: for wide is the gate, and broad is the way, that leadeth to destruction, and many there be which go in thereat: because strait is the gate, and narrow is the way, which leadeth unto life, and few there be that find it.*

A fool tries to avoid danger by shutting his eyes to it, the method by which modern Universalists and modern infidels try to escape hell. They shut their eyes to it or deny its existence. A wise man avoids danger by opening his eyes wide and getting out of the paths that lead to the danger. I will advocate that method from this platform tonight. I am sometimes said to be a man without mercy or a man without a sweet and forgiving nature, because I tell you plainly the peril you are in. Friends, I do not want any of those wonderfully merciful people around me who reveal their sweet and forgiving nature by throwing sand into my eyes and trying to make me think I am safe when I am in grave and imminent peril. The man who points out my sins and my peril is my best friend and my kindest friend. The man who flatters and deceives me is my worst foe and my cruelest foe. Delilah coddled Samson while she bound him for his foes. That is what these so-called liberal-minded preachers are doing. God forbid that for the sake of popularity I should join them in their damnable work of destroying unwary souls.

> The man who points out my sins and my peril is my best friend and my kindest friend.

I shall therefore point out to you with plain speech some of the paths that lead to perdition, in the hope that at least some of you who are walking in these paths will get out of them before you leave this building.

Suicide

The shortest path to perdition, the straightest and quickest road there, is suicide. Judas Iscariot took this road, and the Bible tells us that he went *to his own place* (Acts 1:25). If anyone wants to be in perdition in a few hours, let him take an overdose of morphine or bichloride of mercury. If he wants to be there in a few minutes, let him take carbolic acid. If he wants to be there in a second, let him blow his brains out. There is little hope in the hereafter for a person who commits suicide unless he is truly insane and irresponsible for his foolish and wicked act.

I do not know how many men and women have told me that they intended to commit suicide. To each one I have said, "You will go to hell if you do." I have no doubt that my words were true. To anyone in this audience who is being swept away by the epidemic of suicide that is engulfing us, and is contemplating "solving the mystery of eternity" in that way, I wish to tell you that suicide is the shortest and swiftest road to hell known to man. And there is no getting out of hell after you once get in.

A man who was in great mental anguish once came to me in Chicago. He told me that it seemed as if he must end his life. I told him what would be the certain consequence if he did, and then I pointed out a better way, the way of faith in Jesus Christ. A short time later I met that man again. His countenance was radiant. He had found rest in Jesus Christ.

Impurity

Impurity is sweeping more men, women, boys, and girls into utter destruction in this city than any other sin. Drunkenness claims but a small fraction of the many victims claimed by impurity. The spread of impurity in our land because of the war, and the breakdown of parental restraint at home is appalling. Impurity also increases from lack of sound moral teaching and discipline in our schools and the general outbreak of lawlessness in all areas of our modern life. The sowing of the seeds of infidelity in schools, colleges, and even in Sunday schools and churches everywhere is alarming.

The things I have personally known about the impurity in young and old and in all classes of society have made my heart sick and faint. I know some things about many of you in this audience tonight that you do not think I know. Some I know by your very looks; you bear the marks of your sin in your eyes, in your face, in your gait, and in your manner. Some things I know by direct testimony. Much of our Los Angeles life is festering with the sin of Sodom. Sins of impurity in their various forms are a swift and sure road to perdition. Impurity leads to perdition in many ways.

First of all, impurity breeds unbelief in God, in Christ, and in the Bible. I have found by personal investigation that much of the unbelief of our day has its origin in impurity of life. Let me give you an example. A young student came to me and said that he was skeptical. I asked, "Why are you skeptical?" He replied that he had been reading philosophy, and the study of philosophy had made him skeptical. Then I said, "Is your life right?" He hesitated. I followed it with, "Are you not living in sin?" Then I named the sin I had in mind. He confessed it. I told him to quit his sin and then do certain other things, and he would find that his skepticism would find wings and fly away. He promised to do it. Some months passed. This young man came to me again, and I said to him, "Where do you stand now?"

Impurity breeds unbelief in God, in Christ, and in the Bible.

"Just where I did," he replied.

I asked, "Why have you not gotten over your skepticism?"

"I do not know," he said.

"Have you given up your sin as you promised to do?"

He dropped his head and answered, "No."

"Well," I said, "give up your sin and you will get rid of your skepticism. That's your trouble."

He dropped his head lower and said, "I guess it is."

Yes it was, and it is the trouble with a good many of you men and women here who flatter yourselves that your trouble is skepticism. No, with many of you the real trouble is not skepticism, it is simply disgusting impurity of life. I say that in all kindness and for your own good. If I am correct, do not get angry at me, for I am your friend. Get angry at yourself, for you are your own worst enemy. Get angry at yourself and quit your sin.

Professor W. W. White was once lecturing in Chicago on infidelity. A fine-looking, gray-haired man with a bright mind came up at the close of his lecture and said something like this: "You are a Christian, and I am an infidel. I am just as sincere as you are, and you have no right to tell me I am not."

"Is your life pure?" Professor White inquired in reply.

"Just as pure as yours," the man replied.

"Have you any objection to giving me your name?" Professor White inquired. "I want to look up your record."

The man began to edge away and refused, saying that his name was none of Professor White's business. But Professor White secured his name from someone in the crowd, for he was one of the best-known infidels in Chicago, indeed one of the best-known infidels in America. In less than a year, this gifted infidel was found dead in a Boston hotel, side by side with a brilliant young woman (not his wife) whom he had led astray, first into infidelity, and then into adultery. Impurity makes more infidels than all the infidel books that were ever written. Mind you, I do not say all skeptics and infidels are impure. God forbid! But I do say that impurity makes many infidels. Now you know whether you are impure or not. If you are, and are also an infidel or a skeptic, give up your sin and see how quickly you get rid of your soul-destroying infidelity.

But impurity sends men and women to perdition in still another way. It entangles people in relationships that are hard to get out of but that they cannot remain in and be saved. How many a poor, blinded fool of a man has become infatuated with some other man's wife and run away with her, only to wake up someday and see that both he and she were in hell now and on the way to an eternal hell hereafter. But what could he do? The man who trifles with another man's wife (or trifles with another woman while he has a wife of his own) is not only one of the vilest, most scoundrelly, most contemptible and abject sneaks and villains that walk the face of God's earth, but he is also one of the most complete fools.

I dealt personally one night with a bright, intelligent young man. He was under deep conviction of sin. He told me he wanted to come to Christ. "Well then, why don't you come?" I asked. No answer. Then I looked steadily at him, and his story was revealed. "Is there a woman in the case?" I asked.

"Yes."

"Will you give her up?" There was an awful struggle, a long struggle, but finally he shook his head and walked out to his companion in sin and to hell.

Hell will be crowded with adulterers and adulteresses. Hell will be more full of adulterers and adulteresses than Reno, Nevada. Some of you men here tonight may well tremble. I am not going to point you out, but God knows you. Oh, I appeal to every man and woman here who is taking their first steps on the path of impurity, and also to you who have gotten further on that road, and even to you who are way down that road: Repent, repent, repent, and believe in Jesus Christ tonight. If you do, this will be the happiest night you ever saw.

The Love of Money

The next path to perdition is the love of money. God says, *They that are minded to be rich fall into a temptation and a snare and many foolish and hurtful lusts, such as drown men in destruction and perdition* (1 Timothy 6:9 ASV). How many there are in Los Angeles who are taking this road to hell. Go out to any of our finest avenues; how many saved men are there on it? Very few. Why? Their love of money keeps them from Christ.

But the rich are not the only ones who desire to be rich. Many people in very moderate circumstances are as eager to be rich as the multimillionaire, only they have not been as successful in acquiring wealth. The love of money sends men to perdition in a variety of ways.

First, the love of money leads to dishonest methods of acquiring money. A great many business methods of the present day are simply legalized robbery. Many rich men would have to pay back most of their money to the persons from whom they have stolen it if they were genuinely converted. Some try to get around this by giving away a part of their stealings to churches, colleges, hospitals, public libraries, various Christian organizations, and the poor. This may soothe their own consciences, but it will not satisfy God, and it will not keep them out of hell.

> The love of money leads to dishonest methods of acquiring money.

Again, the consuming love for money blinds many men to the fact that there is anything worth striving for except money, so they leave their souls and their eternal interests utterly neglected. The average lover of money is seldom seen inside a church. There is a great deal more hope of awakening a man intoxicated with whiskey to the fact that he has a soul to save than there is of awakening a man intoxicated with the love of money. I would rather undertake the job of bringing a rum-soaked man to Christ than of bringing a money-soaked man to Christ.

Then again, many who love money, when they are awakened to the fact that they have a soul and that it is lost, will not come to Christ for fear they will have to give their money up if they do. A man once came to Dr. McArthur of New York and said, "Dr. McArthur, must I give up my money if I become a Christian?"

Dr. McArthur replied wisely and said, "If you become a

Christian and Jesus Christ tells you to give up your money, you must be ready to give it up, every penny of it."

The man answered, "I will take a week to think about it." At the end of the week, he came back and said, "Dr. McArthur, I have settled it. I will hold on to my money till death, and if Christ and heaven must go, they must go."

You may say that man was a great fool. I grant it; but there are many others like him, some of them right here in this audience tonight, even if they aren't willing to say it.

Love of Pleasure

Love of pleasure is another path to perdition. Many people in this audience are rejecting Christ Jesus because they think that an acceptance of Christ would involve giving up many pleasures which they are extremely fond of, and very likely it would. Many young people are saying, "I don't think a person can be a real Christian and dance or go to the theater or to the movies or play cards." Well, I admit that I think there is a good deal of truth in what they say. "Well then," they say, "I will hold on to my dancing, or theater, or movies (or whatever it may be), and let Jesus Christ go." They would rather dance to hell than walk with a glad, Spirit-filled heart to heaven. Alas, poor fools!

When I was holding meetings in Nashville, Tennessee, there were four ladies' colleges in that city, and a great many of the students came to the meetings. I think all but three of the young women who were not already Christians in one of the colleges accepted Christ at those meetings, and all but two in another, and I think everyone in another. A large section of the Ryman Auditorium was reserved for them each night. One night one of the colleges had a very large group of students present in one of the galleries to the left of the platform. When I gave the invitation, a large number of those young women rose and afterwards made a public confession of their acceptance of Christ. But one prominent young woman, one of the great social leaders of the college, said after she got back to the college, "If I can't escape hell without giving up my dancing, then I choose to go to hell."

It was an awful thing to say, and you may never put it as bluntly as that, but some of you are acting on that principle. I am glad to say that within a short time that young woman changed her mind and accepted Christ; she became one of the great leaders in the work. I hope that some of you tonight will be equally sensible and change your minds.

Infidelity

Infidelity, or unfaithfulness, is another path to perdition. There is no hope for the unbeliever unless he gives up his infidelity. God tells us plainly that *at the revelation of the Lord Jesus from heaven with the angels of his power in flaming fire, rendering vengeance to them that know not God, and to them that obey not the gospel of our Lord Jesus: who shall suffer punishment, even eternal destruction from the face of the Lord and from the glory of his might* (2 Thessalonians 1:7-9 ASV). And the Lord Jesus Himself says, *Go ye into all the world, and preach the gospel to the whole creation. He that believeth and is baptized shall be saved; but he that disbelieveth shall be condemned* (Mark 16:15-16 ASV).

And we read again in John 3:36 (AKJV) that *he that believeth on the Son hath everlasting life: and he that believeth not the Son shall not see life; but the wrath of God abideth on him.* There is not the slightest chance for an infidel. But you say, "I cannot help being an infidel." Yes you can. If you will come to me, I will show you how to help it. If you are really in earnest, I will show you a way, a way that will commend itself to your own reason and conscience out of infidelity and into faith. I have shown it to many unbelievers, and it has never failed yet.

One of the passages I quoted above, 2 Thessalonians 1:7-9, tells us that it is not only the agnostic and infidel who is on the road to perdition, but also, that all *that obey not the gospel of our Lord Jesus . . . shall suffer punishment, even eternal destruction from the face of the Lord and from the glory of his might.* There are many who in their intellectual opinion about God and the Bible and Jesus Christ are perfectly sound, but who are unbelievers in the biblical sense of unbelief, and every form of unbelief is a path to perdition. They *obey not the gospel of our Lord Jesus,* and therefore by the plain declaration of God's Word, they are on the road to *eternal destruction.* What does it mean to obey the gospel of our Lord Jesus? The Greek word translated *obey* in this passage means first of all "to listen" or "to hearken," and then it means to do what is the result of listening to a command – "obey it." So, to *obey the gospel of our Lord Jesus Christ* means to listen to the gospel, believe what it says, and do what it commands. What does the gospel say?

Paul tells us in 1 Corinthians 15:1, 3-4 (ASV): *Now I make known unto you brethren, the gospel which I preached unto you. For I delivered unto you first of all that which also I received: that Christ died for our sins according to the scriptures; and that he was buried; and that he hath been raised on the third day according to the scriptures.* That, then, is the gospel or good news. The gospel says first that *Christ died for our sins;* believe that. Believe that Jesus Christ died for your sins and trust God to forgive you because Jesus Christ died in your place.

Believe that Jesus Christ died for your sins and trust God to forgive you because Jesus Christ died in your place.

Secondly, the gospel says that Jesus Christ *hath been raised on the third day;* believe that and trust this risen Savior, who has all power in heaven and on earth to deliver you from the power of sin. Then *do* what the gospel tells you to do: confess Jesus Christ before the world. Paul puts it this way: *Because if thou shalt confess with thy mouth Jesus as Lord, and shalt believe in thy heart that God raised him from the dead, thou shalt be saved: for with the heart man believeth unto righteousness; and with the mouth confession is made unto salvation* (Romans 10:9-10 ASV).

Also, confess your renunciation of sin and your acceptance of Christ as your personal Savior by being baptized in His name. The refusal or neglect to obey the gospel by not believing what it says and by not doing what it commands leads to certain perdition. This same thought is found in John 3:36 (AKJV): *He that believeth on the Son hath everlasting life: and he that believeth not the Son shall not see life; but the wrath of God abideth on him.*

Reliance upon a Mere Profession of Religion

Another path to perdition is reliance upon a mere profession of religion. Jesus Christ Himself makes that very plain in the same chapter from which our text is taken. He says, *Not every one that saith unto me, Lord, Lord, shall enter into the kingdom of heaven; but he that doeth the will of my Father who is in heaven. Many will say to me in that day, Lord, Lord, did we not prophesy by thy name, and by thy name cast out demons, and by thy name do many wonderful works? And then will I profess unto them, I never knew you: depart from me, ye that work iniquity* (Matthew 7:21-23 ASV). A man may be a church member and still be on the straight road to hell. A man may have his name on the church rolls (either Protestant or Roman Catholic), be a church officer, be active in various church enterprises, and be a priest or a preacher, but if he has not been born again, he is not saved. If he has not obeyed the gospel and accepted Christ

Jesus as his personal Savior and Lord in such a real way that Christ is transforming him into His own image, that man is still unsaved and is on the road to perdition. He will spend eternity there unless he repents and accepts Jesus Christ with a living faith. Oh, you who are building your hopes of heaven on the fact that you are members of a certain church – Roman Catholic, Methodist, Episcopal, Baptist, Presbyterian, or the Church of the Open Door – if that is all you have to build upon, you are on a path that ends in hell, and you may not be far from your destination.

Putting off Your Acceptance of Jesus Christ

Just one more path that leads to perdition is putting off your acceptance of Jesus Christ to some future time. Many of you know that the path you are now on leads to perdition, and you fully intend to get off that path sometime, but you say, "Not just yet, not tonight."

My friend, that path of delay is one of the surest roads to hell and one of the most crowded. More people go to hell by that road than by almost any other. I suppose that more people in the past who sat in this building but who are in perdition tonight went by this path of putting off, putting off, and putting off a decision than by any other road. If we were to go into the world of those who have died without Christ and ask the people who once lived in this city how they got to that dark world where they now exist, I suppose the great majority would say, "I got here by putting off accepting Jesus Christ." That is what many of you are doing now. You are saying, "I will accept Christ sometime, but not tonight." Listen to what God says: *Boast not thyself of tomorrow; for thou knowest not what a day may bring forth* (Proverbs 27:1). *He that being often reproved hardeneth his neck shall suddenly be destroyed, and that without remedy* (Proverbs 29:1).

An active Christian young man some years ago was urging a friend to accept Christ. "Oh no," he said. "I like to go to the theater; I love to hear Nat Goodwin and some other players. I won't become a Christian yet." The young man urged him to decide for Christ at once and told his friend that there was great peril in delay. In a few days the man who refused to accept Christ at once was not at his place of business, and the Christian young man called on him. There seemed to be nothing very serious the matter with him. He had injured his leg slightly. And still he put off accepting Christ. In a few days, the Christian young man was horrified to learn that his friend was dead. Delay had done its work. Delay had sent another soul to perdition. "Oh," you say, "Dr. Torrey, don't try to frighten us." Listen, I would much rather be frightened into heaven than laughed into hell.

> Jesus Christ is the road, and He is the only road to salvation, to sonship, and to eternal life.

Let me reason with you; let me talk to you as intelligent men and women. Quit right now all these paths that lead to perdition and get on the narrow road that leads to eternal life right now. Take Jesus Christ tonight. He says, and He tells the truth when He says it, *I am the way, the truth, and the life: no one cometh unto the Father, but by me* (John 14:6 AKJV). Jesus Christ is the road, and He is the only road to salvation, to sonship, and to eternal life. Will you take that road now by taking Him?

Chapter 11

There Is a Hell, and If You Don't Look out You Are Going There

And if thy right eye causeth thee to stumble, pluck it out, and cast it from thee: for it is profitable for thee that one of thy members should perish, and not thy whole body be cast into hell. (Matthew 5:29 RV)

For this message, I have five texts. The first is quoted above. The second is Matthew 10:28 (ASV): *Be not afraid of them that kill the body, but are not able to kill the soul: but rather fear him who is able to destroy both soul and body in hell.*

The third is Matthew 23:33 (ASV): *Ye serpents, ye offspring of vipers, how shall ye escape the judgment of hell?*

The fourth is Matthew 25:41 (ASV): *Depart from me, ye cursed, into the eternal fire which is prepared for the devil and his angels.*

The fifth is Matthew 25:46 (ASV): *And these shall go away into eternal punishment: but the righteous into eternal life.*

A very large proportion of the men and women in America today do not really believe that there is a real and awful hell. Indeed, a very large proportion of the ministers and members of orthodox churches today do not believe that there is a real

139

and awful hell. I say they do not "really believe" that there is a real and awful hell. Theoretically, I presume the vast majority of ministers and members of churches do believe that there is a hell. That is, if you put to them the question, Do you believe there is a hell to which the wicked are sent after death (or after the return of the Lord Jesus)? they would say yes. But their belief is not a real belief, a belief that grips them, a belief that shapes their lives and conduct, a belief the meaning of which they realize and that moves them to the action that they would put forth if they really believed it. There is a vast difference between a mere opinion and a real faith. I held the opinion that there was a hell long before I really believed that there was a hell. And I suppose a very large proportion of those who are not professing Christians hold the opinion that there is a hell of some kind in the next world, though perhaps not an everlasting hell, but their opinion is not a real faith. It has very little if any effect upon their conduct.

There is a vast difference between a mere opinion and a real faith.

This widespread loss of belief in a future hell of long and awful sorrow, pain, anguish, remorse, and despair is responsible for many of the terrible evils that are sweeping over our land at the present time. The loss of belief in such a future hell is responsible for the appalling increase in suicides. If men and women believed that every man or woman who committed suicide (unless they were insane and therefore irresponsible) was going to an awful hell, an agelong if not everlasting sorrow, pain, agony, anguish, and despair, suicide would cease instead of increasing at the appalling rate it has increased in the last year. However great their sorrow in the present life, they would not jump from a lifelong frying pan into an everlasting fire. Loss of real belief in an awful and long, long hell is largely responsible for infatuated men and women killing the woman or man they love who does not reciprocate that love, and then killing themselves. If these men and women really believed that such an act meant an eternity in hell, surely not one of them would do it.

This loss of belief in an awful, eternal hell is at least somewhat responsible for every hold-up, burglary, murder, and all this frightful crime wave that is sweeping over this land from New York to Los Angeles. If these men and women who are unhesitatingly staining their hands with blood to get money by open or covert murder realized that their actions meant an eternity in hell, the crime wave would subside into a great calm of righteousness in a day. A reestablishment of real belief in hell as the Bible and Jesus Christ plainly teach would do more to lift our land out of the awful chaos of crime and terror into which it has fallen. A belief in hell would do more than all the increase and improvement of police forces that can be devised, and all the enactment of more severe and better-executed laws that can be imagined.

The loss of man's belief in hell is responsible for the sickening and appalling increase of divorce, legalized adultery, and the ruin that comes to homes and children through it. If men and women who seek divorce because they tire of their spouse or feel their temperaments are incompatible realized their violation of God's law, they would not do so. If they have wickedly permitted their affections to be carried captive by someone other than their lawful wife or husband, and then realized that it was a violation of the law of God and that the demands of decency meant an eternity in hell, this intolerable evil would cease at once.

One of the greatest needs of our day is a restoration of real belief in the teaching of Jesus Christ concerning hell. If we could get men, women, and children in general to believe what Jesus Christ plainly teaches about hell, there would be a general cessation of crime, vice, divorce, suicide, and a general turning of men, women, and children to Jesus Christ as their Savior and Lord and example. I have no expectation of getting men, women, and children *generally* to believe in hell, but I do expect to get many of you here to really believe in hell.

So to get you to quit your crimes if you are criminals, as some of you likely are, and to get some of you who are living double lives and are untrue to wife or husband to quit your vile and damning sin, and to get some of you who are contemplating divorce to give up the thought of that which is pretty sure to land you in an everlasting hell if you do it, and to get every one of you who may be contemplating suicide to give up this silly, cowardly, and desperate act you are planning, an act that will take you to an everlasting hell by lightning express, I hope to lead you to accept Jesus Christ as your personal Savior, surrender to Him as your Lord and Master, and confess Him publicly before the world. This is the only course of action that will save you from spending eternity in the everlasting fire, which was never intended for you but was *prepared for the devil and his angels,* but to which all those who prefer to cast in their lot with the devil rather than to accept Jesus Christ will certainly go.

It Is Certain That There Is a Hell

The first thought I wish to impress indelibly upon your minds, to impress so indelibly and vividly upon your minds that it will determine your whole future conduct, is that there is a hell. Not only is there a hell of suffering and torment of conscience in this life as the consequence of sin, but there is also an awful hell hereafter in the life which is to come, which is the only sense in which Jesus Christ ever speaks of hell. We talk of hell on earth, but that is only an expressive figure of speech; the real hell, the hell of the Bible, is after the present life is ended. It is certain that there is a hell hereafter. Why do I say so?

First, it is certain that there is a hell beyond the grave awaiting vast multitudes now living unless they repent, because Jesus Christ says so. He says so in the plainest unmistakable language in every one of the above texts. I have purposely taken every one of my texts not from the Bible in general but from the words of Jesus Christ Himself. It was easy to do this because Jesus Christ has more to say about hell than any other person whose words are recorded in the New Testament. Jesus Christ had more to say about hell than Peter or Paul or James or John or Jude or all of them put together.

Two Greek words are translated *hell* in our Authorized King James Version. One of them does not properly mean "hell" at all but "hades," the abode of all departed spirits both good and bad up to the time of the ascension of Jesus Christ. At that time the spirits of the righteous dead were taken out of their part of hades – paradise, up into a heavenly paradise, but the wicked were left in their part of hades – Tartarus. They will remain there until the judgment of the great white throne at the end of the millennium, when they will be *cast into the lake of fire,* the real hell.

There is a third Greek word, used once in the New Testament, which is translated *hell* in both the Authorized King James Version and the Revised Version (2 Peter 2:4), but which strictly speaking does not mean "hell" at all, but "tartarus," that part of hades where the wicked dead and some of the fallen angels now are *reserved unto judgment.* After that, they too will be cast into the *lake of fire prepared for the devil and his angels,* the proper hell.

Now the Greek word properly translated *hell* is found twelve times in the New Testament, and in eleven out of those twelve instances it is used by Jesus Christ Himself. Only in one instance is it used by anyone else, and that is James. Of course, hell is spoken of in numerous other passages where the word is not used, but most of these passages also are utterances of Jesus Christ. So to preach hell is to be Christlike in your preaching. In the face of these facts, how utterly silly to say, as so many do, that they are too kindhearted and too full of love for their fellow man to believe in or preach hell. Who was the kindest-hearted man that ever walked this earth? Who was the most full of love of any man who ever walked this earth? Beyond question Jesus Christ is the One who preached hell more than any other New Testament writer or speaker.

What about the men who say it is cruel to preach hell and try to accuse the kindheartedness of John Calvin and Jonathan Edwards? These men were both among the greatest thinkers the world has ever known, and they faithfully presented the truth about hell. Whom are you really accusing? You are accusing Jesus Christ. But Jesus Christ's love for men was of the genuine sort, and He proved His love in a more real and practical way than by lulling men to sleep with false hopes. He didn't play to the spectators to win the praise of empty-headed men by telling them how kindhearted and liberal they are, and how good they are, and how they are not sinners. He didn't tell them that there is a spark of divinity in all of them and that they are in no danger of going to hell. Neither did He tell them that there isn't any hell anyway and that they can get drunk, commit adultery, divorce their wives, oppress the poor, live luxuriously, take life easy while others starve, reject the Son of God, and still come out all right in the end.

Men and women, why do you listen to these ministers of

the devil, masquerading as ministers of righteousness? In your heart of hearts, you know that they are lying to you and lulling you to sleep by false hopes that will land you in an eternal hell. No, Jesus Christ showed His love, real love, genuine love, not camouflaged selfishness, by telling us the truth about hell. He showed His love by leaving heaven with all its glory, coming down to earth with all its shame, and dying the awful death of Calvary, where He bore the awful weight of our sins to save us from going to the hell He had told us about.

Listen to Jesus Christ. You will if you are not a poor, blinded fool. The preacher who declares that there is no hell hereafter or no very awful and long-enduring hell is the most useful servant the devil has in this present dispensation. He is the devil's best servant. Of course, Colonel Ingersoll declared often and with great eloquence that there was no hell. But no really intelligent and fair-minded man or woman ever took Bob Ingersoll seriously. They know he was talking for many hundred dollars a night, and his private morals and private conversations were not of a character to give force to his words in public.

But men do take ministers seriously. Many excellent men and women think anything their minister says must be so. And often the personal morals and private conversation of this class of preachers is so exemplary as to commend their doctrine, and so they beguile many, mislead many, and encourage many to continue in sin and go to hell. Therefore, I say again, don't listen to them; listen to Jesus Christ and then you are safe. What does Jesus Christ say?

Listen to my first text: *And if thy right eye causeth thee to stumble, pluck it out, and cast it from thee: for it is profitable for thee that one of thy members should perish, and not thy whole body be cast into hell* (Matthew 5:29 RV). These are the words of Jesus Christ, and they are from the Sermon on the Mount; I have given you the Revised Version. I have taken these words from the Sermon on the Mount for two reasons. First, because they exactly suit my purpose and state in a plain and unmistakable way the important truth I am trying to make you see and feel. I have taken them from the Sermon on the Mount for a second reason, and that is because most everybody says they believe that part of the Bible even though they do not believe the rest of the Bible. These words are taken from that part of the Bible which most people profess to believe.

I have taken these words from the Revised Version for two reasons. In the first place, I took them from the Revised Version because the Revised Version is a more exact rendering of the original than the Authorized King James Version. And I have taken them from the Revised Version in the second place, because there are many people, including some alleged scholarly preachers, who say that "the Revised Version has done away with hell." That shows how little they know about the Revised Version; there is still plenty of hell left in our texts. It is true the Revised Version does translate one word as *hades* that the Authorized King James Version translates as *hell,* and it is abundantly warranted in doing so. But where the Lord Jesus really spoke about hell, we find it in the Revised Version just as strongly as in the Authorized King James Version. Now these words of our Lord Jesus Christ clearly teach there is a hell into which men are cast after death, and that hell is so awful that it'd be better to suffer any conceivable, lifelong, earthly loss than to go there.

If there is no hell after death, or if the hell after death is not a place of inconceivable agony, then the Lord Jesus was either a colossal fool or a shameless liar. If there is no immeasurably awful hell after death, then either Jesus Christ thought that there was anyway, in which case He was a colossal fool, or He knew that there was not, but taught that there was, to scare men into doing what He wanted them to do, in which case He was a shameless liar and a stupendous fraud. You cannot deny a hell after death of immeasurable agony and horror without making Jesus Christ out to have been a colossal fool or a shameless liar and stupendous fraud.

But Jesus Christ was not a colossal fool; He was not a shameless liar, and He was not a stupendous fraud. He was a teacher sent from God who spoke the very words of God; He was the only begotten Son of God; He was God manifest in the flesh. That was His claim, and God Almighty set the stamp of His endorsement upon that claim by raising Him from the dead. The resurrection of our Lord Jesus Christ from the dead is the best proven fact of history, and that indisputable fact proves Jesus Christ to have been a teacher sent from God who spoke the very words of God. Therefore we must believe whatever He says. And He says that there is a hell after death, a place of conscious torment. Its loss and agony are so inconceivably terrible that it'd be better to suffer any lifelong loss here on earth than go there. As Jesus Christ says, it is settled.

> You cannot deny a hell after death of immeasurable agony and horror without making Jesus Christ out to have been a colossal fool or a shameless liar and stupendous fraud.

We know nothing about the future except what Jesus Christ tells us, either directly Himself or through His inspired apostles. The wisest man's speculations and the greatest philosopher's speculations about the future are worthless. You may say, "I don't believe what the Bible says; I think so and so." But your *think so* is not worth the breath you waste in telling it. Your opinion about either heaven or hell, or about the coming of Christ, or about anything else that lies in the future is worth no more than the opinion some man has about the interior of Africa who has never been in the interior of Africa. Your opinion is utterly foolish and futile guessing. The man we want to hear is the man who has been there, the man who knows. Jesus knows. Listen to Him.

Turn to another statement of Jesus Christ on this subject in Matthew: *Be not afraid of them that kill the body, but are not able to kill the soul: but rather fear him who is able to destroy both soul and body in hell* (Matthew 10:28 ASV). Here Jesus tells us that hell is a place to which both soul and body go. The body does not go to hades; the soul goes there. It may have some temporary body there, but this body that we now inhabit lies in the ground and disintegrates. But at the end of the thousand years, Jesus will raise the bodies of the wicked dead, the righteous dead having already been raised at His coming; but at the end of the thousand years the wicked dead shall hear His voice and come forth. Their bodies will be raised, and soul and body will both be cast together into hell to suffer and spend eternity there (Revelation 20:11-15).

Even in this present life, sin has physical penalties.

It is evident from these verses that according to the teaching of Jesus Christ, hell is a place of physical torment as well as of mental anguish, of remorse, and of shame. The physical agonies of hell are not the worst agonies of hell, but they constitute a very important part of its misery.

Even in this present life, sin has physical penalties. What awful physical suffering I have seen men undergo as a direct consequence of their wrongdoing. It will be so in a greatly enhanced degree in hell.

Listen to a third statement of Jesus Christ: *Depart from me, ye cursed, into the eternal fire which is prepared for the devil and his angels* (Matthew 25:41 ASV), and a fourth: *And these shall go away into eternal punishment: but the righteous into eternal life* (Matthew 25:46 ASV). Here the word *hell* is not found, but the fact of hell is set forth in vivid and appalling language, and it is Jesus Christ who is speaking. We see something of the awfulness of the suffering of hell, and we see the everlasting duration of hell.

The question arises, Does the word *eternal* used in both verses 41 and 46 mean "never-ending"? To this I would say that the word, according to its etymology, might mean simply "age-lasting"; but according to its unvarying usage in the New Testament, it does mean "everlasting." I have shown this in my pamphlet "The Real Truth about an Everlasting Hell." But, furthermore, the word *eternal* is used twice in verse 46. In the first instance, it is coupled with the word *punishment,* and in the second instance, it is coupled with the word *life.* Now what it means in one case, it must mean in the other, because certainly our Lord Jesus Christ was no mere trickster in His use of words. Therefore He would not use the very same word in one part of a verse but with an entirely different meaning in another part of the verse where it is used to contrast. So what the word *eternal* means in connection with *punishment,* it must also mean in connection with *life,* and what it means in connection with *life,* it must also mean in connection with *punishment.*

Now everyone knows that the life that is the reward of the righteous is endless. Therefore, according to the teaching of Jesus Christ, the punishment of the lost must also be endless. Never accept any interpretation of any passage that inevitably involves making Jesus Christ out to have been a contemptible trickster in His teaching.

Someone may ask, Does the *fire* here mean literal fire? We will not stop to argue that now. If you take it as a figure of speech, remember that figures always stand for facts, and since Jesus was no liar, the figures He uses never overstate the facts. How terrific, how appalling must the facts be that warrant Jesus using such a figure as this.

It is certain that there is an everlasting hell because Jesus says so. We have exactly the same reason for believing in a future hell for the wicked as we have for believing in a future life of blessedness for the righteous – God's word uttered by God's own Son. There is no other conclusive proof for either heaven or hell. Give up belief in hell, and if you are logical, you must give up belief in heaven or any future after death. Give up your belief in hell, such a hell as Jesus taught, and logically nothing remains but annihilation for everybody.

But if you are logical, you will not give up one or the other. Jesus Christ taught both, and the known facts about His resurrection from the dead, and many other things also, compel us to accept Jesus Christ as a teacher sent from God, absolutely reliable and inerrant, who spoke the very words of God. It is certain, then, that there is a hell after death. Its agonies are so appalling that it would be better to suffer any loss or pain than go where the body and soul both share in its suffering, and its agonies are so awful as to warrant the figure of *eternal fire* (if it be a figure) in speaking of them, and its suffering never ends.

If there were time or necessity, I could show you that if there is any future life at all, it is certain that there is an awful and eternal hell because every fact of experimental psychology, every dictate of unprejudiced reason, and every known fact of God's present dealing with man points that way. The only thing against such belief is an appeal to prejudice and mere baseless sentiment, an irrational dwelling upon, or drawing unwarranted inferences from, some statements in Scripture. These inferences flatly contradict other plain statements of the same Bible. There is nothing more certain about the future than that there is an awful and eternal hell beyond the grave for many.

If You Don't Look Out You Will Go There

Now a few words about the second part of our subject. The first part of our subject was that there is a hell. We have seen that that is certain. The second part was, if you don't look out, you will go there. Nobody will escape hell without a conscious effort, without deliberate action, without doing one specific thing. We all deserve to go to hell, for we have all sinned, and God is an infinitely holy God. There is not a man or woman here, young or old, who has not sinned. *For all have sinned, and come short of the glory of God* (Romans 3:23 AKJV). *If we say that we have no sin, we deceive ourselves, and the truth is not in us. If we say that we have not sinned, we make him [God] a liar, and his word is not in us* (1 John 1:8, 10).

We all deserve to go to hell, for we have all sinned, and God is an infinitely holy God.

There is not a man or woman here tonight who has not sinned outrageously; there is not a man or woman here tonight who has not broken God's first and greatest commandment and thereby committed the greatest sin a man or woman can commit. What is God's first and greatest commandment? Listen to the words of Jesus again: *And he [Jesus] said unto him, Thou shalt love the Lord thy God with all thy heart, and with all thy soul, and with all thy mind. This is the great and first commandment* (Matthew 22:37-38 ASV). This is God's first and greatest commandment – to love God with all your heart, with all your soul, and with all your mind. That is to put God first in everything – God first in business, God first in politics, God first in home life, God first in social life, God first in amusements, and God first in study.

Not one of us has ever done this our whole life through. Therefore, every one of us has broken this first and greatest of God's commandments, and therefore every one of us has committed the greatest sin a man or woman can possibly commit. We all deserve to go to hell, and we will go to hell unless we make some definite effort and take some definite step to keep from going there. No one ever drifted to heaven. Anyone who merely drifts, drifts to hell. Many of you here tonight are merely drifting.

I once saw a little card. On one side of the card was this question: "What must I do to be saved?" Then God's own answer to the question was given as found in Acts 16:31 (ASV): *Believe on the Lord Jesus, and thou shalt be saved.* At the bottom of the card it said, "Turn over." And turning it over, I found this question: "What must I do to be lost?" It gave the answer in one word: "Nothing." One does not need to do anything to be lost. We are lost already unless we do something definite.

If you are on the Niagara River, way up above the falls and the rapids, and you just drift, you are bound to go over the falls. You do not need to take up the oars and pull with the stream in order to go over the falls. The way to keep from going over the falls is to pull upstream, and you must begin pulling before you get into the rapids. Well, we are in the current of sin, and the current is moving toward hell – at first slowly, but soon faster, and at last with a rush that cannot be resisted. Consent to drift and you are sure to wind up in hell. If you don't look out, you will go there.

In what way must we beware in order not to go there? What must we do to keep us from going to hell? There is only one thing we can do that will keep us from going to hell. Anyone who does that one thing will escape hell and go to heaven; on the other hand, anyone good or bad, vicious or moral, liberal, generous or outrageously miserly, lovely and amiable, or mean and disgusting, anyone who does not do that one thing will go to hell. What is that one thing? The answer is found repeatedly in the Word of God: Accept Jesus Christ as your Savior. Read what God says: *He that believeth on him is not condemned: but he that believeth not is condemned already, because he hath not believed in the name of the only begotten Son of God*

(John 3:18 AKJV). *As many as received him, to them gave he the right to become children of God, even to them that believe on his name* (John 1:12 ASV). *He that believeth on the Son hath everlasting life: and he that believeth not the Son shall not see life, but the wrath of God abideth on him* (John 3:36 AKJV).

We have all sinned, as we have seen, and therefore are hellward bound. But Jesus Christ died for our sins. *All we like sheep have gone astray; we have turned every one to his own way; and the LORD hath laid on him the iniquity of us all* (Isaiah 53:6 AKJV). He made perfect atonement for our sins, and then He rose from the dead and lives today. He has all power in heaven and on earth; therefore, He has power to give us victory over sin every day. Accept Him as your atoning Savior, who settled every one of your sins by dying for them on the cross. Trust God to forgive you because the Lord Jesus died in your place; the moment you do it your sins are all forgiven. *Be it known unto you therefore, brethren, that through this man is proclaimed unto you remission of sins: and by him every one that believeth is justified from all things* (Acts 13:38-39 ASV). Trust Him also as your risen Savior to keep you from the power of sin, and He will. Do that and you will be saved; don't do it and you will spend eternity in hell. Really doing it involves surrendering your life, your thoughts, your will, and your conduct to His control. It involves the open confession of Him before the world. Real faith always leads to open confession. As Paul puts it: *Because if thou shalt confess with thy mouth Jesus as Lord, and shalt believe in thy heart that God raised him from the dead, thou shalt be saved: for with the heart man believeth unto righteousness; and with the mouth confession is made unto salvation* (Romans 10:9-10 ASV).

What are you going to do? Are you going to choose heaven

> He has all power in heaven and on earth; therefore, He has power to give us victory over sin every day.

or hell? Will you accept Christ tonight and make sure of heaven? Or will you reject Christ and make sure of hell?

Chapter 12

Heaven Is Real, and Whoever Wishes Can Spend Eternity There

In my Father's house are many mansions; if it were not so, I would have told you; for I go to prepare a place for you. And if I go and prepare a place for you, I come again, and will receive you unto myself; that where I am, there ye may be also. And whither I go, ye know the way. Thomas saith unto him, Lord, we know not whither thou goest; how know we the way? Jesus saith unto him, I am the way, and the truth, and the life: no man cometh unto the Father, but by me. (John 14:2-6 ASV)

As in the previous message, I am using five texts here. My second text is John 17:24 (AKJV): *Father, I will that they also, whom thou hast given me, be with me where I am; that they may behold my glory, which thou hast given me: for thou lovedst me before the foundation of the world.*

My third text is Hebrews 8:1 (ASV): *Now in the things which we are saying the chief point is this: We have such a high priest, who sat down on the right hand of the throne of the Majesty in the heavens.*

My fourth text is 2 Corinthians 5:1 (ASV): *For we know that if the earthly house of our tabernacle be dissolved, we have a building from God, a house not made with hands, eternal, in the heavens.*

My fifth text is 1 Peter 1:3-5 (ASV): *Blessed be the God and Father of our Lord Jesus Christ, who according to his great mercy begat us again unto a living hope by the resurrection of Jesus Christ from the dead, unto an inheritance incorruptible, and undefiled, and that fadeth not away, reserved in heaven for you, who by the power of God are guarded through faith unto a salvation ready to be revealed in the last time.*

My subject in the previous message was that there is a hell, and if you don't look out, you are going there. We saw that it was absolutely certain that there was a hell after death; its agonies were so appalling that it would be better to suffer any loss or pain than go there. We also saw that body and soul both shared in its suffering and its agonies that are so awful as to warrant the figure of speech of *eternal fire* (if it be a figure) in speaking of them; its suffering never ends. And we saw that it was certain that we would go there unless we did one specific thing – accept Jesus Christ as our personal Savior, which involves the surrender of ourselves to Him as our Lord and Master, and open confession of Him before the world.

Tonight we turn from this very dark and forbidding subject to a very bright and alluring subject: namely, there is a heaven, and whoever wishes can spend eternity there. Last Sunday night I confined my texts to statements of Jesus Christ, because men naturally are unwilling to believe in hell, and for many people, the words of Jesus Christ have more weight than the words of Paul or John or other New Testament writers. Indeed, with any really intelligent, fair-minded, and genuinely logical man who faces the facts in the case, the words of Jesus Christ must be absolutely conclusive and decisive. When Jesus Christ says anything, the matter is settled for any man who is not a fool.

I know that there are those who pose as great scholars and do not accept the statements of Jesus Christ as final, but that only shows how a man can be a great scholar and at the same time be a great fool. We all know that the history of human thinking abounds in instances where great scholars have been proven to be great fools. In fact, through the whole history of human scholarship, the "assured results" of the scholarship of one generation have continually proven to be the exploded nonsense of the next generation. Every generation of scholars admits that about the scholarship of preceding generations, but each generation cherishes the hope that it will not prove true of their generation. They imagine that they at last have attained the "final science" and the "absolute philosophy."

> When Jesus Christ says anything, the matter is settled for any man who is not a fool.

Well, that is what our dear departed ancestors thought about the science and philosophy of their day, but it did not turn out that way. And our descendants will be making merry over our scientific and philosophical follies, just as we are now making merry over those of the scholars who have passed on. But amid the wreck of human scientific theories and human philosophies, the words of Jesus Christ stand unmoved and unassailable. Every man who is really wise believes His words absolutely, and the man who does not may imagine that he is a philosopher, but he had better spell the first syllable with two o's rather than one i (phoolosopher).

Tonight I start with two foundational texts that are from the words of Jesus Christ, but I also use texts from others who were unquestionably inspired by God, texts that illuminate and emphasize the words of Christ.

The Absolute Certainty That There Is a Heaven

The first thought I wish to drive home and so rivet in your minds that you will never question it again is that it is absolutely certain that there is a heaven to which certain persons are going. I am as certain that there is such a place as heaven as I am that there is such a place as Los Angeles. Why is it absolutely certain that there is such a place as heaven?

First, it is absolutely certain that there is such a place as heaven because Jesus Christ says so. He says so in the first of our texts. He says, *I go to prepare a place for you.* He does not say, "I go to prepare a state or condition for you." He says, *I go to prepare a place for you,* and when our Lord Jesus says *place,* He means *place.* All this modern clamor about heaven being a condition or a state of mind has no authority in the words of Jesus Christ nor in anything else in the Bible. Of course, it would be better to be in a heavenly moral condition and a heavenly state of mind in a decidedly unheavenly place, than to be in a hellish moral condition and hellish state of mind in a heavenly place. But it is better to be in a heavenly moral condition and heavenly state of mind in a heavenly place, and that is what is ahead for us if we meet the conditions that I shall state later.

Yes, heaven is a place. We are not going to be disembodied spirits in our eternal condition any more than Jesus Christ today is a disembodied spirit. His spirit, His real, essential personality, was disembodied for three days and three nights. He left His body on the cross and went down into hades, but after three days His body was raised. We have seen again and again from this platform that this is the best proven fact of history, and His spirit returned to that body and took that resurrected, transformed, and glorified body up to heaven with Him.

Stephen saw Him in His body after His ascension (Acts 7:55-56), and Saul of Tarsus saw Him after His ascension. He is in a bodily form tonight, in a place we call heaven. We too shall have bodies and be in a place, and that place is heaven. You may like this disembodied-spirit stuff, but I do not. As I read Sir Oliver Lodge's *Raymond*, and the descriptions given by the alleged spirit of his son through various spiritualistic ascetics of the life he was living since his death, I thought to myself, I cannot see what comfort Sir Oliver Lodge gets out of that. If that is the heaven of Spiritualism, I would just as soon that my son should be in hell, and much rather that he would be annihilated and utterly cease to be.

But that is not the heaven Jesus Christ teaches, nor is it the heaven of actual fact. Heaven is a real place, and no one who goes there will have any desire to come down and hover around darkened, uncanny rooms to contact his friends through some low-living medium, who is usually a drunkard or a dope fiend. Many of them are notoriously immoral, and all of them are of a low type of mentality.

> Heaven is a real place, and no one who goes there will have any desire to come down and hover around darkened, uncanny rooms to contact his friends through some low-living medium.

Jesus Christ emphasizes the fact that heaven is a place by the first statement in the same verse when He says, *In my Father's house are many mansions,* that is, many "abiding places" as distinguished from the transitory character of our earthly homes. I had a home in Montrose, Pennsylvania. It was as beautiful and comfortable a home as I desired in this world. My wife was tired of wandering about Europe, Asia, Africa, Australia, and America, and wanted to settle down, so I bought this home. We thought it would be our home for the rest of our earthly lives. She said, "Let's call it *Alabama*," which means "Here we rest." And we called it Alabama, and we rested, or she did. How long? Less than four years, and here we are way out in California, and in a few months from now, we will be in Asia again. But in the next world, we have a *continuing city* as God calls it in Hebrews 13:14 (AKJV). The Revised Version translation is *an abiding city*. The Greek word translated *abiding* is the participle of the verb from which the noun translated *mansions* in John 14:2 is derived. Heaven is a place – a permanent place. Yes, heaven is a place.

Furthermore, Jesus says, *I go to prepare a place.* Evidently, He was going from a place where He then was, Jerusalem, on this earth, to another place where He was soon to be. What was that place? John 14:28 (ASV) answers the question. Jesus said, *Ye heard how I said to you, I go away, and I come unto you. If ye loved me, ye would have rejoiced, because I go unto the Father.* Here Jesus says, "I am going away from where I now am and where you are. I am going away from you to my Father," that is, God. Well, where is God? Turn to the Lord's Prayer as found in the Sermon on the Mount, and Jesus will tell you just where God is. That prayer which our Lord taught us begins with the words *Our Father who art in heaven* (Matthew 6:9 ASV). That is where God is; He is *in heaven*. Of course, God is everywhere in His Spirit, but that is only one side of the truth. God has a local habitation, and that habitation is heaven. That is where God is, and that is where our Lord Jesus Christ is now – at His right hand. That is where Stephen saw Him (Acts 7:55-56). That is where we are going someday. Somebody heard that I was going to China next summer, and he asked me if I'd take him along as a private secretary. Let me tell you, before long, I am going to a much more interesting place than China. I am going to heaven, and any of you can go along if you wish. I will tell you how before I finish here.

In other places in the Sermon on the Mount, our Lord Jesus tells us that heaven is a place, and that God the Father is there. He tells us so in Matthew 7:11 (AKJV): *If ye then, being evil, know how to give good gifts unto your children, how much more shall your Father which is in heaven give good things to them that ask him?* And in Matthew 7:21 (AKJV) He says, *Not every one that saith unto me, Lord, Lord, shall enter into the kingdom of heaven; but he that doeth the will of my Father which is in heaven.*

Our Lord Jesus tells us in another of our texts that heaven is a place, a glorious place, and that all those who will believe on Him are going there. Listen again to John 17:24 (AKJV): *Father, I will that they also, whom thou hast given me, be with me where I am; that they may behold my glory which thou hast given me.* If there is anything that Jesus teaches over and over again and is therefore absolutely certain, because there is no possibility of doubting what Jesus taught, it is that there is a heaven, and that heaven is a place. He teaches that God is there in a sense that He is nowhere else, and that Jesus is now there, and all who really believe in Him are to be there someday.

In the second place, it is certain that there is a heaven, not only because our Lord Jesus says so, but also because those who have been unmistakably proven to have been inspired of God say so.

Paul says in 2 Corinthians 5:1 (ASV), *For we know that if the earthly house of our tabernacle be dissolved, we have a building from God, a house not made with hands, eternal, in the heavens.* The house of God that Paul speaks of here refers, as the context plainly shows, to our glorified resurrection body, the body made in the likeness of our Lord's own glorified body (Philippians 3:21). And Paul tells us that body is not only *eternal* but also *eternal, in the heavens.* That body will exist elsewhere eternally, and where that body will exist eternally is *in the heavens.*

Peter also tells us that there is a heaven, and it is a place. *Blessed be the God and Father of our Lord Jesus Christ, who according to his great mercy begat us again unto a living hope by the resurrection of Jesus Christ from the dead, unto an inheritance incorruptible, and undefiled, and that fadeth not away, reserved in heaven for you, who by the power of God are guarded through faith unto a salvation ready to be revealed in the last time* (1 Peter 1:3-5 ASV).

Here Peter tells us that heaven is a place, and in that place there is an *inheritance incorruptible, and undefiled, and that fadeth not away,* securely kept there for all those who are kept by the power of God through faith unto that glorious *salvation ready to be revealed in the last time.* People are wondering in these days of bank looting, high-power explosives, and Bolshevik uprisings where they can store their possessions with absolute safety. Well, there is no place on this earth where you can store them with absolute safety. Even if they do not succeed in blowing up your safe or your safety-deposit vault, you may die any day. Then you cannot get your possessions, and someone else will get them, probably the lawyers. But if they are *reserved in heaven,* they are absolutely safe. People sometimes want to know if you have your money in a Federal Reserve Bank. Better to have it in the *heavenly* reserve bank. If it is there, not only can neither moth nor rust corrupt, nor thieves break through and steal, but furthermore, there is also no power either in earth or hell to rob you of it. It is absolutely, eternally safe. And what a glorious inheritance it is – *incorruptible, and undefiled, and that fadeth not away.* It is more specifically described in Romans 8:17: *heirs of God, and joint-heirs with Christ,* heirs of all that God has and all that God is. It is better to give up anything and everything on earth and get heaven, than to get everything on earth – great wealth, beautiful homes, high-powered automobiles, diamonds and gems, operas, theaters, and dances – but lose heaven. Do you know how I feel when I ride by the palatial homes of some of our very rich and godless millionaires or when I sometimes enter them? I do not have a feeling of envy at all; I feel a great pity – so rich today and utter paupers tomorrow, paupers for all eternity.

The author of the epistle to the Hebrews also teaches that there is a heaven and that it is a place. It makes no difference whether Paul is the author of this epistle to the Hebrews or someone else; the book is inspired of God in either case. It bears the marks of its inspiration on every page. It differs radically from all the other literature outside the Bible, of that time or any other time. It has the unmistakable inspired flavor. Listen to what God says in Hebrews 8:1 (ASV): *Now in the things which we are saying the chief point is this: We have such a high priest [Jesus Christ], who sat down on the right hand of the throne of the Majesty in the heavens.*

God teaches us here that there is a heaven (or heavens), that it is a place, that His own throne is there, and that Jesus is there. Elsewhere in this same book, He tells us that we are going there too, if we are Christ's. He tells us that Christ has entered heaven as a *forerunner* (Hebrews 6:20); that is, He has gone there before us, and we are to follow after.

It is certain, then, that there is a heaven because Jesus Christ says so, and because men who beyond an honest doubt were inspired of God, men through whom God Himself spoke, say so. That settles it. As I stated last night, we know absolutely nothing about the eternal future except what God has been pleased to tell us through His Son, Jesus Christ, and through His inspired servants, the writers of the New Testament. That is sure; all else is mere guesswork and baseless speculation. What the philosophers, the speculative theologians, or the scientists guess about heaven or hell is of no more value that what an inmate of an insane asylum guesses about them. The philosophers and scientists are entirely out of their sphere concerning the future.

A story is told of a distinguished man of science who had to cross a ferry in a rowboat. As the man at the oars pulled him across, the scientist said to him, "Do you know astronomy?"

"No," replied the rugged oarsman, "I do not."

"Well then," said the man of science, "a quarter of your life is gone. Do you know anything about geology?"

"No."

"Then one-half of your life is gone. Do you know anything about biology?"

"No."

"Then three quarters of your life are gone." Just then the boat struck a snag and flipped. As they plunged into the water, the oarsman cried, "Do you know how to swim?"

"No."

"Well then, your whole life is gone," and the ferryman struck out for shore, but the great scientist drowned. He was out of his element. When mere scientists and philosophers begin speculating about the eternal future, they are out of their element, and they flounder around and drown, unless they will let someone who knows his Bible pull them ashore. What the scientist or philosopher speculates about heaven or argues about heaven is pure and simple guesswork and worthless; what God says through His Son through the inspired writers of the Bible is true. It is sure, then, that there is a heaven and that heaven is a place. It is a wonderful place, and God is there, Christ is there, and many of us are going there. We can all go there if we so desire.

What Kind of a Place Is Heaven?

Now what sort of a place is heaven? Some think that we know nothing about it, and all is guesswork. They quote 1 Corinthians 2:9 (AKJV) to prove it: *Eye hath not seen, nor ear heard, neither have entered into the heart of man, the things which God hath prepared for them that love him.* But they stop too soon. They should quote the next verse: *But God hath revealed them unto us by his Spirit: for the Spirit searcheth all things, yea the deep things of God.* We know nothing about heaven except what God has revealed, but God has been pleased to reveal a great deal about heaven.

I think very few Christians realize how much God has told us in the Bible about heaven. I think few Bible scholars realize how much God has told us about heaven. I have studied this subject more or less for many years, but when I took it up again last Monday, I confess that I was surprised to find so much about heaven in the Bible. What God, who made heaven and who lives there, has told us about heaven in the Bible, and what God has revealed to us about heaven through His Son in the Bible, is not only very interesting but also immensely cheering. It is calculated to awaken in every wise and sensible heart an intense desire to go there. But we don't have time to go into that at length now. Just this hasty summary without any attempt to cite the passages or to expound at length will suffice for now.

1. *Heaven is a place of matchless, inconceivable, external, material, and visible beauty.* I love beauty, and it has been my good fortune to see a large share of the most renowned beauty spots of Europe, Asia, Australasia, and America. I have sat for hours just drinking in the beauty of some of these places. But nothing I have ever seen – in Japan, China, India, Australia, or New Zealand, or Yosemite, the Grand Canyon of the Colorado River, the Alps, the Rockies, Loch Lomond, or at Ben Nevis – can compare for one moment to the beauty and majesty and sublimity and glory of that land beyond the shadows, the matchless city of God.

2. *Heaven is a land of indescribable harmony, melody,*

and music. They have a choir of one hundred million voices there (Revelation 5:11), and every voice sweeter and richer than Caruso's, and no orchestra on earth can match those "harpers harping with their harps."

3. *Heaven is a place of countless wealth.* Every inhabitant is a multimillionaire, *heirs of God, and joint-heirs with Jesus Christ* (Romans 8:17).

4. *Heaven is a place unmarred by sin.* In heaven God's will is perfectly done by all, and where nothing that defiles mind or affections or will shall ever enter.

5. *Heaven is a place where there is no trace of sickness or twinge of pain.* Heaven is where death never enters, and where no tear is ever shed.

6. *Heaven is a place of highest, holiest, and most ennobling companionships.*

7. *Heaven is the place where God is, where His Son, Jesus Christ, is, and where we shall be with Christ and with God the Father, and we shall see his face* (Revelation 22:4). Oh, to see the face of God! Moses wanted to see the face of God, but he was told that no man could see His face and live (Exodus 33:20). But with the strength of our resurrection bodies and perfectly redeemed spirits, we can gaze and gaze and gaze upon that wonderful face of God and live. I wonder if, when God took Moses up onto Mount Nebo to die, He didn't let Moses have his prayer answered at last and see His face and then die, die a death of immeasurable ecstasy. But in that world, we shall see His face and live and be satisfied! Oh, how profoundly significant are the

words of the psalmist in Psalm 17:15 (ASV): *I shall be satisfied, when I awake, with beholding thy form.*

Anyone Who Wishes Can Spend Eternity in Heaven

Now just a few words on the last part of our subject: Anyone who wishes can spend eternity in heaven. Why do I say that? Because our Lord Jesus says so. He says so in our first text. He says, *Whither I go, ye know the way.*

And then Thomas said unto Him, *Lord, we know not whither thou goest; how know we the way?*

Then Jesus replied, *I am the way, and the truth, and the life: no man cometh unto the Father, but by me.* Here He says that He Himself is the Way to heaven, and anyone who takes Him takes the way to heaven. If you take Him and start to heaven, you are bound to get there. He says also in John 10:9, *I am the door: by me if any man enter in, he shall be saved. If any man,* mind you, no exceptions. The poorest are as welcome as the richest, the most ignorant are as welcome as the wisest, the vilest sinner is as welcome as the finest saint. *If any man.* Come along, friends.

> The poorest are as welcome as the richest, the most ignorant are as welcome as the wisest, the vilest sinner is as welcome as the finest saint.

Peter also tells us the same thing in our last text: *Blessed be the God and Father of our Lord Jesus Christ, who according to his great mercy begat us again unto a living hope by the resurrection of Jesus Christ from the dead, unto an inheritance incorruptible, and undefiled, and that fadeth not away, reserved in heaven for you, who by the power of God are guarded through faith unto a salvation ready to be revealed in the last time* (1 Peter 1:3-5 ASV).

That is all: *who by the power of God are guarded through faith.* It is not a question of our puny strength but of His almighty strength, given to all who believe on His Son. Believe in Jesus Christ, that is all. All God's children are certainly going to spend eternity in the Father's house, and John 1:12 (ASV) tells us how to become children of God: *But as many as received him, to them gave he the right to become children of God, even to them that believe on his name.* Just accept Jesus, that is all. Accept Him as your personal Savior, the One whom God Himself tells us bore all your sins in His own body on the cross. Trust God to forgive all your sins because the Lord Jesus died in your place. Accept Him as your risen Savior who now lives in heaven and has all power in heaven and on earth; therefore, He has power to keep you every day and hour; just trust Him to do it. Accept Him as your Lord and Master to whom you surrender the entire control of your thoughts and life; confess Him as your Lord before the world, and you will spend eternity in heaven. Refuse to accept Him, or neglect to do so, and you will spend eternity in hell.

There is a heaven, and whosoever wishes can spend eternity there. Do you wish to do that? It is up to each one of you tonight to say for yourself whether you will spend eternity in heaven or eternity in hell. Which do you choose? Oh, unless you are a poor, blinded fool you, will choose to spend eternity in heaven. Then accept the Lord Jesus Christ right now. You may say, "I do not want to do it right now, but I will do it at some future time." Take no chances. Hell is too awful to take any chance of going there, and heaven is too glorious to take any chance of missing it. There is only one thing for any man or woman to do who has the least spark of wisdom left but has not already accepted Jesus Christ. Accept Jesus Christ and confess Him tonight.

Chapter 13

The Day of Golden Opportunity

The Holy Spirit saith, Today. (Hebrew 3:7 ASV)

T he day of golden opportunity is today. Golden opportunities, opportunities of priceless worth, are open to every one of us today. But tomorrow has no sure promise for any one of us. *The Holy Spirit saith, Today,* and conscience also cries, "Today," and the voice of reason, the voice of history, and the voice of experience unite in one loud chorus and shout, "Today." Only the voices of apathy, laziness, and folly murmur, "Tomorrow." The Holy Spirit is calling, "Today." Men in their folly are forever saying, "Tomorrow."

When the frightful plague of frogs came upon Pharaoh and upon his people, in his terror Pharaoh sent for Moses and Aaron and said, *Entreat Jehovah, that he take away the frogs from me, and from my people; and I will let the people go, that they may sacrifice unto Jehovah* (Exodus 8:8 ASV).

Moses replied, *Against what time shall I entreat for thee, and for thy servants, and for thy people, that the frogs be destroyed from thee and thy houses, and remain in the river only?* (v. 9).

One would naturally suppose Pharaoh would have answered,

"At once," but Pharaoh, like many other kings, played the fool and answered, *Against tomorrow* (v. 10).

Men show a similar folly and often a greater folly today. When urged to forsake sin with its miseries, degradation, and perils, and turn to Christ with the joy and peace and ennobling of our character and security that He gives, they answer, "Yes, I think I will."

"When?"

"Oh, tomorrow." But *the Holy Spirit saith, Today.*

A poor wretch came into my office one day. He had been drinking, and drinking had brought misery into his heart and ruin into his life. I asked, "Will you quit drinking and turn to Jesus Christ?"

"Oh," he exclaimed, "there is nothing else that I can do, so I will."

"Will you do it now?"

He hung his head and murmured, "Not now, tomorrow." But *the Holy Spirit saith, Today.* Tomorrow is the devil's day and the fool's day. Today is God's day and the wise man's day.

I wish to give you some conclusive and unanswerable reasons why every man and woman in this auditorium who makes any pretense to intelligence and common sense should not only accept the Lord Jesus as his Lord and Savior but should also accept Him here before he leaves this building tonight, if he has not already done it. What I want to get is action, immediate action, intelligent and wise action. And the only action that is intelligent and wise for anyone who has not already accepted Jesus Christ is to accept Him right here now. Resolutions to do the right thing and the wise thing at some indefinite time in the future are of no value whatever. God's time is now. *The Holy Spirit saith, Today.*

The Lord Jesus Brings Peace

The first reason every man and woman in this auditorium who has not already accepted Jesus Christ should not only accept Him but also accept Him now is because the Lord Jesus brings peace to the tormenting conscience as soon as He is accepted. The really wise man will not only desire that peace but also desire it just as soon as he can get it. Wherever there is sin, there will be an accusing conscience. And we know *all have sinned.* If any man has sinned and his conscience does not accuse him and torment him, he has sunk very low. There are, of course, different degrees of torment of conscience and different kinds of torment of conscience. With some, the pain is sharp and piercing, and with some it is dull and grinding, but there is pain; there is unrest; there is no peace in the heart where sin has entered until that sin has been forgiven.

But Jesus Christ gives peace to the most agonized conscience. Men and women have come to me in all degrees of misery over the memory of some sin that they have committed, and I have pointed them to the Lord Jesus. Everyone who has gone to Him has found rest. I can't imagine how many men and women have come to me who were driven to the verge of hopeless despair by the accusations of their conscience. They were contemplating self-destruction in the hope of thus getting away from their mental agony. But I led them to Jesus Christ, and now they have rest and the peace of God that passes all understanding.

Everyone who has gone to Him has found rest.

A young man came to me one Sunday morning in Chicago in awful agony. He had sinned grievously and was reaping the harvest. He was contemplating all sorts of mad recourses to escape the inevitable consequences of his sin. I pointed him to the Son of God, and he accepted Him. Afterwards he brought his companion in sin to me. She was fully determined to do a desperate deed that was likely to land her in prison or in the cemetery. I pleaded with her and pointed her to the real cure – the Savior. When she left me, she was still undecided as to what she would do. Afterwards she decided, and she decided rightly.

One night a long time later, as I was going down the back stairs of the Moody Church to the inquiry room, a young, happy-faced woman stopped me and said, "I want to thank you for what you did for me and for my husband and my child." I did not recognize her for a moment, so she said, "I am the young woman who came to you," and she explained the circumstances. She was the woman who had contemplated the destruction of her child and her own destruction for time and for eternity. But she had found peace in Jesus Christ. Men and women with tormenting consciences and with uneasy, restless hearts, there is rest for you in Jesus Christ. If you are wise you will not only find rest, but you will also find it tonight. *The Holy Spirit saith, Today.* You need not spend even one more day or one more hour in the agony of your accusing, tormenting conscience.

Jesus Christ Brings Joy Unspeakable and Full of Glory

The second reason every man and woman in this auditorium who has not already accepted Jesus Christ should not only accept Him but also accept Him now is because Jesus Christ brings joy unspeakable and full of glory – a joy to which the joy of this world is as nothing in comparison – to everyone who accepts Him as soon as they accept Him and confess Him. Any wise man will not only desire this joy but also desire it at once. I for one not only wish the best I can get, but I wish it as quickly as I can get it. The joy that is in Jesus Christ is the very best joy one can get.

There is not a particle of doubt about that. Ask anyone who

has ever tried the world and has then tried Jesus Christ. You cannot find one single man or woman who has tried the joy that there is in Christ, anyone who has put his trust in Him as his personal Savior and unreservedly surrendered to Him as his Lord and Master, who will not tell you that the world has no joy for a moment comparable with that joy which is found in Jesus Christ. No matter how rare their opportunities may have been for enjoying the world, they will tell you without the slightest hesitation that the joy one finds in Christ is incomparably greater and finer and more satisfying than any joy the world can give. There are millions of witnesses to this fact, and their testimony is unanimous.

I know the joy that comes from wealth; I know the joy that comes from the theater; I know the joy that comes from dances and the card table; I know the joy that comes from the racetrack and the wine supper, and so on to the end of the list of this world's joys. I know also the joy that comes from literature, art, music, science, philosophy, and travel. I know practically every joy that this world has to give, but I say to you tonight that the joy of all these put together is nothing compared to the *joy unspeakable and full of glory* that comes from a genuine acceptance of Jesus Christ as our Savior, and a wholehearted surrender to Him as our Lord. There is joy in a constant and open confession of Him before the world, and from receiving the Holy Spirit whom He gives to those who do accept Him and surrender to Him.

Men and women, if you wish to have the highest, deepest, purest, and most abounding joy, immeasurably the most satisfying joy that is to be known, not only in your future life but also in this life now, come to Jesus Christ; come tonight. *The Holy Spirit saith, Today.*

Jesus Christ Brings Deliverance
from the Power of Sin

The third reason every man and woman in this auditorium who has not already accepted Jesus Christ should not only accept Him but also accept Him tonight is because Jesus Christ brings deliverance from the power of sin. Any wise man or woman not only wishes deliverance from the power of sin but also wishes it as soon as he can get it. There is no other form of slavery known to man so degrading and so wretched as the slavery to sin. It'd be better by far to be the poor black slave of the most brutal black driver the South ever knew than to be the slave of rum, lust, bad temper, dope, impure imagination, greed for gold, or any other form of sin. Poor old Uncle Tom, groaning in his cabin after the cruel blows of the brutal Simon Legree, is not as pitiful an object as a wretch, poor or rich, who is under the scourge of appetite, lust, dope, or any other sin. But there is freedom at hand, right now. Jesus Christ sets men free from sin in all its form. He sets men free who have been slaves for years. He sets them free in a moment. Any sinner here can find deliverance in Christ from any sin and can find it tonight. What Jesus said when He was here on earth is just as true today: *Every one that committeth sin is the [slave] of sin* (John 8:34 ASV). But thank God it is also as true today as when He said, *If therefore the Son shall make you free, ye shall be free indeed* (John 8:36 ASV). Any man or woman here who has a spark of intelligence will not only wish for deliverance from sin and its awful bondage, but will also wish for it at once. What would you have thought of any old-time black slave of a vile and cruel master who had been offered freedom and answered, "Yes, I wish for liberty. My bondage has been awful. But I don't want the freedom just yet. I will wait

Jesus Christ sets men free from sin in all its form.

until next year. I will wait until next month. I will wait until next week. I will wait until tomorrow."

You would exclaim, "What a fool!" But he would not be so colossal a fool as you are when you say, "Yes, I do wish for deliverance from the power of sin," and then add, "but not tonight, tomorrow." Oh men, listen. *The Holy Spirit saith, Today.*

Jesus Christ Brings Beauty of Character

The fourth reason every man and woman who has not already accepted Jesus Christ should not only accept Him but also accept Him tonight is because Jesus Christ brings beauty of character, and every wise man and woman will not only desire beauty of character but also desire it just as soon as they can get it. I sometimes notice advertisements in the papers that read, "The Secret of Beauty." I can tell you the secret of beauty, men and women, the secret of permanent, indestructible beauty. It is Jesus Christ in the heart. He not only beautifies the face, He also beautifies the soul. He makes over the soul that trusts in Him into His own glorious likeness. I have seen some of the foulest men and women I ever knew made over into the fairest, and it was Jesus Christ who did it.

Sam Hadley, of the Water Street Mission in New York, was the friend of all men who were down and out. He was always on the lookout for an opportunity to help some man who was about as bad as they make them get back on his feet and lead him to Christ to get the man saved. A man said to Mr. Hadley one day, "I have a friend whom I wish you would take an interest in."

Sam Hadley asked, "Who is he?"

"He is Bowery Ike."

"Well," said Hadley, "what is he anyhow?"

The man replied, "He is a crook. He makes his living by stealing and picking pockets and all that sort of thing. At present he is on Blackwell's Island, serving a term there. You can find him more easily now than usual."

Sam Hadley went over to Blackwell's Island and found Bowery Ike, for he could not get away; he was behind bars. Bowery Ike had no use for Sam Hadley, except that when he got out, he came around to Sam to get a little money to get a new suit of clothes. But he was soon off to the Island again. Every time he would come out of confinement, he would go around to see Hadley, but as soon as he got on his feet again, he would go back to his crooked work. Sam Hadley followed Bowery Ike for seven long years, and one day at the end of the seventh year, Bowery Ike was thoroughly sick and tired of sin. This time he not only came to Sam Hadley but also came to Jesus Christ too, and Jesus Christ opened His arms and took Bowery Ike in.

After Bowery Ike had been saved for about a year, Sam wrote to me, saying, "Mr. Torrey, I have a man who wants to study at your school. They used to call him Bowery Ike. His right name is Ira Snyder. We believe in him. He has been a tough customer. He has been a hard case. But he is saved, and we believe God wants to use him. Will you take him?"

"Dear Sam," I replied, "I will take anybody you recommend."

He wrote back, "I recommend him."

Then I wrote, "Send him on." And Bowery Ike (Ira Snyder) came. Listen, men. Though that man had been a crook from his boyhood, for he commenced picking pockets when he was just a little lad, he became one of the most beautiful Christians I have ever met in all my life.

And I say to you tonight that I have known thieves who have come to Christ, burglars who have come to Christ, train robbers and bank robbers who have come to Christ, harlots, murderers, and people guilty of every kind of crime I ever heard of who have come to Christ and have become some of the loveliest Christians I have ever known. Yes, some of the men and women who were once down in the deepest depths of sin.

But to come back to Ira Snyder, Bowery Ike, he came to Chicago. He stayed with us about a year, a little over a year. One night he said to me, "I want to walk home with you and have a little talk with you." On the way to my home he said, "I made a little visit down in New York a few weeks ago. I think they need me in New York. I have loved it in Chicago, and I would like to stay on, but I believe they need me in New York. I have written Mr. Hadley that I am ready to go back to New York and help in the work."

A few days after this, Ira Snyder was taken down with influenza, a slight attack, not a very serious case, but he went to bed with it. They did not think he was very ill. But as I was leaving the dining table one night, the maid told me that Mr. Hunter, who was one of my assistants at that time, wished to see me. I met Mr. Hunter, and he said, "Mr. Torrey, Ira Snyder is dead."

I said, "What, John? You don't mean Ira Snyder?" We had another man at the Institute at the same time whose name was much the same, who was very ill at that time too. I thought Mr. Hunter must mean him. "You don't mean Ira Snyder," I said, "you must mean So-and-so," naming the other man.

"No," Mr. Hunter said. "Mr. Torrey, Ira Snyder is dead. He died very suddenly about an hour ago."

I asked, "Where is he, John?"

"He is over at the undertaker's. They have prepared him for his burial and have placed him in his coffin. They are going to have the service tomorrow, and I thought I should come tell you tonight."

"That was right, John," I replied. "Let's go over." We went to the undertaker's, which was not far away, and walked into the parlor. And there in a beautiful coffin lay Ira Snyder. When I looked down into that face, one of the noblest faces I have ever looked into in my life, I will tell you what I did. I could not help it; I broke down, and leaning over I kissed Ira Snyder's beautiful face as he lay there in his coffin. Yes, friends, Bowery Ike had been a crook before he became a Christian, but by the power of Jesus Christ in his heart, he became one of the loveliest Christians I ever knew in my life. I don't think my heart ever ached over anybody outside my own family as it did over Ira Snyder. He was formerly a pickpocket, a burglar, and everything that was bad, but in his lost and ruined condition, he came to Jesus, and the heart of Jesus was big enough to take him in. Jesus came into his heart and transformed him into His own likeness. The Lord Jesus is doing that sort of thing every day.

The Lord Jesus is also taking others who are not as foul, who indeed the world thinks are fair, and He is making them immeasurably fairer. It is Jesus and Jesus only who makes truly lovely characters. Ah, men and women, don't you wish to be fair? Not only fair in the eyes of man but also fair in the eyes of God? You could be. It is Jesus' work to make you so. Let Him begin at once. Let Him begin it tonight. *The Holy Spirit saith, Today.* What do you say? Tomorrow? No, not if you have a particle of sense left, and I believe you have. You will say, "Tonight. Right now."

Jesus Christ Fills Our Lives with Highest Usefulness

The fifth reason every man and woman in this auditorium who has not already accepted Jesus Christ should not only accept Him but also accept Him tonight is because Jesus Christ fills our lives with highest usefulness, and every wise man and every wise woman desires not only to be useful but also to begin being useful as soon as possible. The Christian life is the only really useful life. We look at the life of many a one who is

178

not a Christian and say, "There is a useful life." But God looks at it and looks through it; He looks at it in all its bearings and writes this verdict upon it: "Useless."

Whether you and I see it or not, the man or woman who is not with Christ is against Him (Matthew 12:30), and the man who is against Jesus Christ is against God and against humanity. His life is useless and worse than useless. But the life that is fully surrendered to Jesus Christ becomes a useful life at once. It may be the mere wreck of a life, but it becomes a useful life at once.

A friend of mine found one of the most hopeless wrecks of womanhood in New York City and brought her to Jesus Christ. I think this poor creature lived less than two years after her conversion, and many months of that time were spent upon a sickbed. But that woman was used for the eternal salvation of more than a hundred persons while she lay there dying. The story of the transformed life of "the Bluebird of Mulberry Bend" has gone around the world and saved thousands.

Come to Christ. Really come to Him. He will make you useful. Come at once so your usefulness can begin at once. I am glad I came to the Lord Jesus when I did, but oh, if I had only come sooner. How many precious years were wasted! How many golden opportunities were lost, opportunities that will never return. Come, men and women. Come now. *The Holy Spirit saith, Today.*

The Sooner We Come to Christ, the Fuller and Richer Will Be Our Eternity

The sixth reason every man and woman in this auditorium who has not already accepted Jesus Christ should not only accept Him but also accept Him tonight is because the sooner we come to Christ the fuller and richer will be our eternity. The eternity of each one of us will be what we make it in this life. You are constructing your eternity every day. Every day of true service for Christ makes our reward so much the greater and our eternity so much the fuller and richer. Come to Christ next Sunday, and you will be behind for all eternity by as much as you might have done this week. You may cry in coming years, "Backward, turn backward, O Time in thy flight," but time will not turn backward in its flight. Time cannot turn backward. Time is flying by every moment and never returns. Today is hurrying by at express speed. Tomorrow will soon follow. And as I turn around and peer after yesterday and today as they plunge into the unfathomable depths of the past, I cry, "Yesterday, where are you?"

Out from the fathomless abyss of bygone days comes the answer: "Gone forever."

And I hear the Holy Spirit crying, "Today! Today! Today!" *The Holy Spirit saith, Today.*

If We Do Not Come to Jesus Christ Today, We May Never Come at All

One more reason that every man and woman in this auditorium who has not already accepted Jesus Christ should not only accept Him but also accept Him tonight is because if we do not come to Jesus Christ today we may never come at all. That is not at all a remote possibility. Thousands and tens of thousands have been as near to an acceptance of Jesus Christ as you are tonight and have said, "Not tonight." But they have passed without Christ into that world in which there is no hope for repentance, no matter how diligently with tears we may seek it, into that world in which there is no opportunity to change our mind or our eternal destiny.

A man came into one of our tents one night in Chicago. It was the first time he had ever been in a meeting of that kind in his life. The words of Mr. Schiverea, who spoke that night, made a deep impression upon him. After the meeting was over, he lingered with a friend and talked personally with Mr. Schiverea. His friend accepted Christ, and he was on the verge of accepting Him also. Mr. Schiverea said to him, "You will accept Jesus Christ right now?"

"No," the man said. "This is the first time in my life that I was ever in a meeting of this kind. I cannot decide tonight, but I promise you that I will come back Sunday night and accept Christ."

It was Friday night, and there was to be no meeting on Saturday. Mr. Schiverea replied that he did not question at all the honesty of his intention or the sincerity of his promise to return Sunday night and settle it, but he added, "We have no guarantee whatever that you will live until Sunday night."

"Oh," the man said, with a laugh, "you don't suppose that God is going to cut me off after the first meeting of this kind that I ever attended in my life and not give me another opportunity?"

Mr. Schiverea replied, "I do not know. But I do know you are taking a great risk in waiting until Sunday night. I greatly fear that if you do not accept Jesus Christ now, you will never accept Him and will be lost forever."

"No," the man said, "I give you my word that I will be back here Sunday night and accept Christ."

Mr. Schiverea continued to plead with him, but the man would not yield. He went out of the tent with his friend. They got into a carriage and turned toward home. And as they drove up the street, they passed a saloon. The man said to his friend, "Let's stop and have one more drink, and then we will both swear off."

"No," said his friend, "I have settled it already. I have accepted Christ, and I will never take another drink."

"Well," said the other, "I'm going to have one more drink anyhow. You drive up the street and then come back for me; I will be waiting for you outside." He entered the saloon. His friend drove up the street, and after a few minutes, returned to pick up his friend. He was nowhere to be seen. He went into the saloon to look for him. He was not there. He went into the street again and looked up and down for his friend, but he was nowhere in sight. Passing a high board fence, he heard a groan, and passing swiftly around behind it, he discovered his friend had been stabbed and was lying with an awful gash in his body, unconscious and dying. He was taken to the Presbyterian hospital and lived until Monday morning, but never regained consciousness and passed into eternity unsaved, lost forever. Why? Because when *the Holy Spirit saith, Today,* he said, "Tomorrow." So he passed unprepared into the presence of God, and so will some of you, if you do not listen to the Holy Spirit tonight, as He *saith, Today.*

One night when I was preaching in Bradford, England, a man and his wife sat side by side in the meeting; they were deeply moved, but they made no decision and gave no sign. As they walked away from the meeting, the wife said to her husband, "Wouldn't it have been nice if you and I both had risen tonight and gone forward together and accepted Christ?"

He answered, "Yes, it would." They reached home and retired. About two o'clock the following morning, his wife awakened him and said, "I feel so strange." In a few minutes from that time, she passed into eternity. After he had laid his wife's body away in the cemetery, he came back to the meeting, told us this story, and accepted Christ, but he came alone. Oh, men and women, listen! Don't you hear the Holy Spirit crying, *Today*?

Many things besides death may make this the last opportunity you will ever have and will make a refusal tonight final and fatal. Loss of opportunity may come. The Holy Spirit is here in power now. It is a great opportunity, the day of golden opportunity. A similar opportunity may never come again. It never will come again for some of you. *The Holy Spirit saith, Today.*

A hardened heart may seal your doom. When a human heart is moved upon by the Spirit of God, as some of your hearts are tonight, and the heart continues to resist the Holy Spirit, it is likely to become very soon hardened and hopeless.

A hardened heart may seal your doom.

One night in our church in Chicago, after the meeting in which many had accepted Christ, I remained talking with a young man. He was under deep conviction, within one step of a decision. I urged upon him an immediate acceptance and confession of Christ. "No," he said, "I cannot do it tonight. But I will give you my word of honor that I will come back tomorrow night and do it."

I told him I did not question his word or his intention, but I said, "I have no guarantee whatever that you will keep your word. I have a feeling in my heart that if you do not settle it tonight, you will never come back."

"Why," he replied, "my mother is here every night. We live within a block of this place. I give you my word of honor I will come tomorrow night and settle it."

Again I said, "I do not question your word, but the Spirit of God is working mightily with you tonight, and if you go out of here resisting the Spirit of God, I believe your heart will be so hardened that your eternal destiny will be sealed and you will never come back."

"No," he said, "I cannot accept tonight, but I will come tomorrow night and settle it."

He walked away. I watched him with a heavy heart as he passed out of the door. I said to myself, "He will never come back," and he never did. Quite a while later I asked his mother about him, and she told me he had never come back into the church after that night.

Men and women, listen! You cannot trifle with God; you cannot trifle with your own souls, and you cannot trifle with the Holy Spirit. The Holy Spirit is not only saying in our text, but he is also saying in your hearts tonight, "Today! Right now! Accept Christ." Will you listen to the mighty, gracious Spirit of God? Will you do as He bids you? Will you listen right now and harden not your heart? Will you accept Jesus Christ as your Savior, surrender to Him as your Lord and Master, and begin to confess Him as such before the world? Will you be saved, and get right with God here and now, and receive the wonderful blessings that He gives and that He alone gives?

Reuben A. Torrey –
A Brief Biography

Reuben A. Torrey was an author, conference speaker, pastor, evangelist, Bible college dean, and more. Reuben Archer Torrey was born in Hoboken, New Jersey, on January 28, 1856. He graduated from Yale University in 1875 and from Yale Divinity School in 1878, when he became the pastor of a Congregational church in Garrettsville, Ohio. Torrey married Clara Smith in 1879, with whom he had five children.

In 1882, he went to Germany, where he studied at the universities at Leipzig and Erlangen. Upon returning to the United States, R. A. Torrey pastored in Minneapolis, and was also in charge of the Congregational City Mission Society. In 1889, D. L. Moody called upon Torrey to lead his Chicago Evangelization Society, which later became the Moody Bible Institute. Beginning in 1894, Torrey was also the pastor of the Chicago Avenue Church, which was later called the Moody Memorial Church. He was a chaplain with the YMCA during the Spanish-American War, and was also a chaplain during World War I.

Torrey traveled all over the world leading evangelistic tours, preaching to the unsaved. It is believed that more than one hundred thousand were saved under his preaching. In 1908, he helped start the Montrose Bible Conference in Pennsylvania, which continues today. He became dean of the Bible Institute of Los Angeles (now Biola University) in 1912, and was the pastor of the Church of the Open Door in Los Angeles from 1915 to 1924.

Torrey continued speaking all over the world and holding Bible conferences. He died in Asheville, North Carolina, on October 26, 1928.

R. A. Torrey was a very active evangelist and soul winner, speaking to people everywhere he went, in public and in private, about their souls, seeking to lead the lost to Jesus. He authored more than forty books, including *How to Bring Men to Christ, How to Pray, How to Study the Bible for Greatest Profit, How to Obtain Fullness of Power in Christian Life and Service*, and *Why God Used D. L. Moody*, and also helped edit the twelve-volume book about the fundamentals of the faith, titled *The Fundamentals*. He was also known as a man of prayer, and his teaching, preaching, writing, and his entire life proved that he walked closely with God.

Other Similar Titles

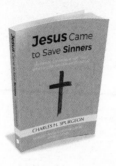

Jesus Came to Save Sinners, by Charles H. Spurgeon

This is a heart-level conversation with you, the reader. Every excuse, reason, and roadblock for not coming to Christ is examined and duly dealt with. If you think you may be too bad, or if perhaps you really are bad and you sin either openly or behind closed doors, you will discover that life in Christ is for you too. You can reject the message of salvation by faith, or you can choose to live a life of sin after professing faith in Christ, but you cannot change the truth as it is, either for yourself or for others. As such, it behooves you and your family to embrace truth, claim it for your own, and be genuinely set free for now and eternity. Come and embrace this free gift of God, and live a victorious life for Him.

Available where books are sold.

The Way to God, by Dwight L. Moody

There is life in Christ. Rich, joyous, wonderful life. It is true that the Lord disciplines those whom He loves and that we are often tempted by the world and our enemy, the devil. But if we know how to go beyond that temptation to cling to the cross of Jesus Christ and keep our eyes on our Lord, our reward both here on earth and in heaven will be 100 times better than what this world has to offer.

This book is thorough. It brings to life the love of God, examines the state of the unsaved individual's soul, and analyzes what took place on the cross for our sins. *The Way to God* takes an honest look at our need to repent and follow Jesus, and gives hope for unending, joyous eternity in heaven.

Available where books are sold.

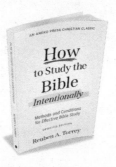

How to Study the Bible Intentionally,
by Reuben A Torrey

Nothing is more important for our own mental, moral, and spiritual development, or for our increase in usefulness, than Bible study. But, not all Bible study is equally profitable. Some Bible study is absolutely profitless. How to study the Bible so as to get the most benefit from it is a topic of immeasurable importance.

The practicality and effectiveness of these Bible study methods and conditions have been tested in the classroom, and not with classes made up completely of college graduates, but largely composed of people of very simple education. The methods, however, require time and hard work. It must be remembered that the Bible contains gold, and almost anyone is willing to dig for gold, especially if it is certain that he will find it. It is certain that one will find gold in the Bible – if he digs. As you use the methods recommended in this book, you will find your ability to do the work rapidly increasing by exercise, until you can soon do more in fifteen minutes than you could do in an hour when you started.

Available where books are sold.

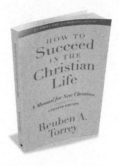

How to Succeed in the Christian Life,
by Reuben A Torrey

"I have for years felt the need of a book to put in the hands of those beginning the Christian life that would tell them just how to make a complete success of this new life upon which they were entering. I could find no such book, so I have been driven to write one. This book aims to tell the young convert just what he most needs to know. I hope that pastors and evangelists and other Christian workers may find it a good book to put in the hands of young converts. I hope that it may also prove a helpful book to many who have long been Christians but have not made that headway in the Christian life that they long for."

– Reuben A. Torrey

Available where books are sold.

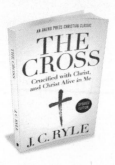

The Cross, by John C. Ryle

I want to tell you what perhaps the greatest Christian who ever lived (the Apostle Paul) thought of the cross of Christ. Believe me, the cross is of deepest importance. This is no mere question of controversy; this is not one of those points on which men may agree to differ and feel that differences will not shut them out of heaven. A man must be right on this subject, or he is lost forever. Heaven or hell, happiness or misery, life or death, blessing or cursing in the last day – all hinges on the answer to this question: "What do you think about the cross of Christ?"

Available where books are sold.

Repentance , by John C. Ryle

It is indifference that leaves people alone and allows them to go their own way. It is love, tender love, that warns them and raises the cry of alarm. The cry of "Fire! Fire!" at midnight might sometimes rudely, harshly, and unpleasantly startle a person out of his sleep, but who would complain if that cry was the means of saving his life? The words Except you repent, you will all likewise perish might at first seem stern and severe, but they are words of love, and they could be the means of delivering precious souls from hell.

Available where books are sold.

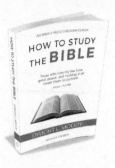

How to Study the Bible, by Dwight L. Moody

There is no situation in life for which you cannot find some word of consolation in Scripture. If you are in affliction, if you are in adversity and trial, there is a promise for you. In joy and sorrow, in health and in sickness, in poverty and in riches, in every condition of life, God has a promise stored up in His Word for you.

This classic book by Dwight L. Moody brings to light the necessity of studying the Scriptures, presents methods which help stimulate excitement for the Scriptures, and offers tools to help you comprehend the difficult passages in the Scriptures. To live a victorious Christian life, you must read and understand what God is saying to you. Moody is a master of using stories to illustrate what he is saying, and you will be both inspired and convicted to pursue truth from the pages of God's Word.

Available where books are sold.

The Kneeling Christian, by Albert Richardson

The Lord Jesus is as powerful today as ever before. The Lord Jesus is as anxious for men to be saved as ever before. His arm is not shortened that it cannot save, but He does stretch forth His arm unless we pray more – and more genuinely. Prayer, real prayer, is the noblest, the sublimest and most stupendous act that any creature of God can perform. Lord, teach us how to pray.

Available where books are sold.

Life in Christ, by C. H. Spurgeon

Men who were led by the hand or groped their way along the wall to reach Jesus were touched by his finger and went home without a guide, rejoicing that Jesus Christ had opened their eyes. Jesus is still able to perform such miracles. And, with the power of the Holy Spirit, his Word will be expounded and we'll watch for the signs to follow, expecting to see them at once. Why shouldn't those who read this be blessed with the light of heaven? This is my heart's inmost desire.

I can't put fine words together. I've never studied speech. In fact, my heart loathes the very thought of intentionally speaking with fine words when souls are in danger of eternal separation from God. No, I work to speak straight to your hearts and consciences, and if there is anyone with faith to receive, God will bless them with fresh revelation.

Available where books are sold.

Pilgrim's Progress, by John Bunyan

Often disguised as something that would help him, evil accompanies Christian on his journey to the Celestial City. As you walk with him, you'll begin to identify today's many religious pitfalls. These are presented by men such as Pliable, who turns back at the Slough of Despond; and Ignorance, who believes he's a true follower of Christ when he's really only trusting in himself. Each character represented in this allegory is intentionally and profoundly accurate in its depiction of what we see all around us, and unfortunately, what we too often see in ourselves. But while Christian is injured and nearly killed, he eventually prevails to the end. So can you.

Available where books are sold.